garden
ornaments

gar
ornar

hamlyn

den
ents

Moira and Nicholas Hankinson

photography by Mel Yates

For Eleanor

First published in Great Britain in 1999 by Hamlyn
an imprint of Octopus Publishing Group Limited,
2–4 Heron Quays, London E14 4JB

© Octopus Publishing Group Limited 1999

Publishing Director Laura Bamford
Executive Editor Mike Evans
Senior Editor Nina Sharman
Project Editor Jo Lethaby

Creative Director Keith Martin
Executive Art Editor Geoff Borin

Production Controller Phillip Chamberlain

Photography Mel Yates

A CIP record for this book is available
from the British Library.

ISBN 0 600 59742 3

The publishers have made every effort
to ensure that all instructions given in
this book are accurate and safe, but
they cannot accept liability for any
resulting injury, damage or loss to either
person or property whether direct or
consequential and howsoever arising.
The author and publishers will be
grateful for any information that will
assist them in keeping future editions
up to date.

Measurements Both imperial and
metric measurements have been given
throughout this book. When following
instrucions, you should choose to work
in either metric or imperial, never mix
the two.

Produced by Toppan Printing Co Ltd
Printed and bound in China

introduction 6

seating and eating 10

mosaic table top 16
decorated chairs 18
cider bench 20
hammock 22
stencilled tray 24
garden lights 26
Somerset trug 28

wind and weather 32

weather vane 38
wind chimes 40
horizontal sundial 42
garden awning 46

birds and wildlife 48

bird nesting box 54
bat box 56
bird table 58
bird bath 62

creative containers 64

terracotta wall planter 70
patio planter 72
window box/planter 74
fish box planter 76
farrier's box 78
orange box planter 80
perfect pots 82

inspirational ideas 90

flowerpot topiary 96
evergreen topiary bird 98
wire heart 100
recycled wall planters 102
garden markers 104
window pane clock 106
slate fountain 108

sources and techniques 100

using colour 112
paints and stains 114
simple finishes 116
timber 118
ageing techniques 120
tools and equipment 120

useful addresses 124
index 126
acknowledgments 128

contents

introduction

above *A 19th-century wooden shop front with original glass rescued from demolition and installed into a recently build walled garden, giving an elegant look to the utilitarian potting shed*

above *A 19th-century cast iron finial positioned as a decorative detail on a reconstructed greenhouse*

right *This stone-cast head water feature gazes down on the tranquil terraced water garden below*

Were you to cast your eyes over the assorted paraphernalia scattered across the half acre "plot" we acquired with our farmhouse just over two years ago, who could blame you for wondering why we of all people had embarked on a book entitled *Garden Ornaments*.

Rusty corrugated iron carbuncles are now so familiar that we have to admit we do not even notice them. Disused and crumbling pig pens; a pile of broken concrete, discarded drain pipes, scattered building stone and an old cracked and chipped porcelain sink, are but a few of our numerous garden "ornaments". Perhaps the one redeeming feature of our garden, apart from the uninterrupted views and the fantastic sunsets, is an ancient stone-lined and rather lovely fresh water well which probably predates the present house. From the time spent thinking and developing the ideas for this book, a very practical blueprint plan for our garden has emerged, a design that is flexible, fun, sometimes flamboyant, formal in part and most importantly, relatively inexpensive to construct and easy to maintain. This plan, in turn, underlies the concepts behind the projects we have selected for the book.

However, this book is not strictly about gardens or gardening, it is about garden ornaments; the furnishings that will complement your outdoor space and, of course, your home, so that the indoor living area and outdoor space merge into one another to fit in with today's casual sophistication and easy relaxed life style. The excess of magazines and books on homes and gardens, as well as television programmes on home and garden improvement, reflects the explosion of creative ideas in these areas.

The aim of this book is to stimulate thoughts and ideas about using your outdoor space as a natural extension of the home, and to provide examples of garden art, accessories, furnishings or ornaments, whatever you like to call them, that can be made inexpensively, using tools and materials you may already have, or are easily available. There are over 30 different projects that are grouped together in themed chapters – Seating and Eating, Wind and Weather, Birds and Wildlife, Creative Containers, and Inspirational Ideas. The projects are suitable for all levels of ability, whether you are a keen novice or have some previous experience in making decorative items for the home or garden and know the satisfaction of having created something with your own hands. The only other requirement is imagination. If you like the ideas but lack the time or inclination to roll up your sleeves and wield a hammer, paint brush or craft knife, *Garden Ornaments* may just persuade you into rethinking and possibly rearranging your outdoor space in order to achieve a grand plan or make a simple statement. We are continually told by the media to revise, edit and update our appearance, our wardrobe and our interiors, so why not our exterior spaces too? Never has there been a better choice of materials, accessories, furniture and indeed plants available to us, from mass-produced high street accessories to bespoke works of art.

Horticulture is now in vogue – the height of fashion. At one end of the spectrum the furnished garden may contain grand and impressive statuary in lead,

bronze or marble, fountains, follies and temples, perhaps even a lake. At the other end, but none the less visually exciting, is the urban back yard, paved and filled with stone urns or terracotta pots and featuring a table and chairs for outdoor entertaining. The soil, plants and planting are only parts of the whole scheme. The other parts are the ornaments and garden props that give the space an element of surprise, that form the theatre and create the atmosphere, since gardens are not natural, but cultivated and essentially artificial. The props should be adaptable to be moved around with the change of the seasons or your change of mood, and the green "room" can be "redecorated" just as you would a room in the house.

Consider linking the colours of your garden with those you have selected in your home and give some thought as to how you will use your exterior space. For example one area may be designed for relaxing in, another used as a working area perhaps for growing vegetables and you may want a designated dining area and space for entertaining. All this can be achieved in even a small garden with a little improvisation and some imagination. Weddings, parties or any other social occasion can be used as an excuse to embellish the garden, possibly creating a thematic extravaganza. Utilize the full potential of your garden to ensure that it is enjoyed all year round.

Outdoor furniture and decorative accessories can add style, atmosphere and visual interest to any exterior space, reflecting the tastes and character of their owners.They can also act as focal points on lawns, patios and in flower beds. Be bold but at the same time keep it simple. Balance shape, texture, light, scale, movement, colour, mass and tone. Emphasize curves and different textures perhaps by lining up old terracotta pots, reclaimed clay tiles or industrial pipes cut down and placed on end. Use unusual combinations of materials such as bleached wood and bamboo, metal, cobblestone, brick, gravel, concrete and mulch for dramatic effects. Be individual, free-spirited, brave and adventurous.

left *A variety of rusted, black-leaded and weathered cast iron garden edgings that have been reproduced from original 19th-century designs*

above *An abundance of old terracotta pots awaiting planting with herbs in a productive kitchen garden*

right *Dovecotes were built with a practical purpose, to provide food for the fledgling squabs during winter. Now redundant, they make attractive focal points in established gardens*

seating and eating

As with any room in the house you need to plan and furnish your exterior space. If you have space, create some hidden, secret areas where a hammock can be hung or a deckchair placed for privacy. Whether your garden involves colourful chaos or minimal landscaping, treat it as a relaxing haven, a restful retreat full of fragrance – perhaps somewhere to sleep to the sound of running water, and to awake to the song of birds.

There can be few pleasures as enjoyable as entertaining friends and family with impromptu meals eaten alfresco. Create an area just for eating, perhaps with a built-in barbecue nearby. Make an unusual garden table from a section of cast-iron flooring salvaged an old greenhouse (see opposite). And don't neglect to plan the lighting for dining after dark.

An outdoor eating area needs to be private, even if this means a location at the end of the garden away from the convenience of the house. Choose somewhere that is out of sight of onlookers, shaded and restful, in a spot filled with flowers and herbs, fruit and fragrance.

Having chosen the site, the style of furniture must also be considered. The furniture in the garden is not an accessory, it should be an integral part of the form, harmonizing with nature so that not only are you able to enjoy a beautiful landscape, but you also become part of it. A hammock slung between two trees is the perfect place on lazy summer days – somewhere to curl up with a good book or just browse through magazines. A rustic bench adapted from a chapel seat, sculpted from figured and weathered oak or simply constructed from slabs of elm rescued from a fallen tree makes a perfect retreat for rest and contemplation.

Outdoor furniture comes in very many designs and a great number of different materials. There are various types of portable garden chairs: campaign and safari chairs and deckchairs come in cotton prints, textured weaves, checks and stripes. Wood is a classic favourite for garden furniture and teak is probably the most commonly used hardwood since it weathers wonderfully to a subtle silvery grey colour, as if it has been washed for years by ocean spray. Reclaimed timbers salvaged from old buildings can also be used very imaginatively. Benches and chairs made in softwood such as pine, which is in plentiful supply and takes paint and stains very well, make versatile "occasional" furniture on which to sit and dine or sip a long, cool, quenching drink.

left *An aged oak garden bench in a sculptor's garden in Devon, England*

above *A pine chapel seat used as a garden bench in a sunny arbour is complemented perfectly by an old French trug and a selection of white-washed and brightly painted flowerpots*

right *Secret seating in a woodland setting, provided by a weathered elm seat made from a fallen tree*

Cast iron, heavy and fashionable towards the latter part of the 19th century, is another alternative for garden furniture and is enjoying a resurgence in popularity. Many of the original Victorian designs have also been copied in lightweight aluminum. Mild steel is another weighty material, that is used for wrought-iron chairs, tables and benches and lends itself to fences and gates bent into fanciful and curlicue shapes.

Rattan, grass and cane are frequently used for furniture in conservatories and garden rooms and conjure up nostalgic pictures of colonial-style covered verandas in the tropics. Another natural material, living willow, can be trained into bowers or arched shapes to make a screen or backdrop for a traditional timber bench. Finally, there is of course inexpensive moulded plastic, which looks good in shades of green, less so in white, and is arguably the most comfortable and easy to maintain of all garden furniture.

Garden seating and eating areas need to be lit once it is dark, and for real atmosphere the most romantic lighting is candlelight. The humble household candle can be used very effectively, placed inside an empty jam jar and grouped with others on a table or around the area to be illuminated. There are many tall candle holders available, designed to be driven into the ground and surmounted by a glass cylinder to protect the flame from wind, as well as many pretty globes, lights, lamps and lanterns to choose from. In this chapter we show you how to make simple lights using candles and unusual materials. Of course, you do have the option of installing outside electricity to give you floodlighting, spotlighting, downlighting, uplighting or even underwater lighting.

Suppose that you now have your boldly painted or decorated table, folding wooden chairs and flickering candlelight by which to dine long after the sun has set. All that is required are the final props, the finishing touches to complete your table setting. Rustic wooden or woven chestnut trugs and trays in traditional earthy colours or willow baskets woven by skilled craftsmen make perfect table displays, filled with fresh or dried flowers, home-made delicacies or small terracotta pots overflowing with garden herbs.

above *An antique cast-iron café table has been given a contemporary look with a verdigris painted finish*

left *Live willow cuttings have been stuck into the ground and trained into a growing arched back for a rustic seat*

right *A table display of driftwood and pots in a hidden corner of a garden*

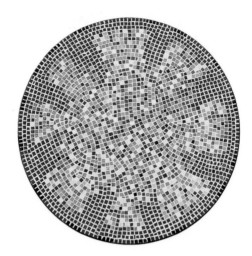

Mosaic is a tradition as old as history. We are familiar with photographs of the ancient mosaics of Pompeii and Herculaneum, which are as invigorating today as when first executed. Mosaic floors in shaded Moorish water-filled courtyards provided an oasis of coolness in dry, sun-drenched environments. In today's gardens, modern mosaic is equally enchanting. It can be used to embellish or decorate floors, walls, furniture or even more mundane domestic items. Illustrated opposite are a number of new terracotta pots enhanced with mosaic decoration, that complement the abstract, garden-inspired design selected for the mosaic table top.

Materials for mosaic can be as diverse as the places in which they are to be used. Tesserae selected from broken china and tiles may just as easily be put to use as the ceramic tile chips purchased from a craft supplier that we used for this project. We have even seen a quite superb table made from pieces of old blue willow pattern china discovered in the owner's garden.

If you decide on a geometric or representational pattern, it is probably best to draw the pattern directly on to the table in pencil and lay the tile pieces on top to fit the design. Very effective and time-saving dual-purpose tile and grout products are now available: these act as both adhesive and grout in the one material.

materials

Waterproof MDF (medium-density fibreboard), chip (particle) board or plywood, at least 18mm (¾in) thick
Tile pieces
Tile adhesive
Waterproof tile grout

equipment

Hand saw
Coarse-grade glasspaper or heavy-duty wire brush
Tile snips
Pencil and paper
Small wooden spatula
Disposable rubber gloves
Rubber spatula
Clean cotton rag

mosaic table top

1 Using a hand saw, cut the board to the shape of the table top required. Ensure the surface is clean and free of dust or grease. If you are using a painted board, sand the surface or roughen it with a wire brush to provide a key for the tile adhesive. If you need to cut your tiles into smaller pieces to provide the detail necessary for the design, use tile snips to cut the tiles into the size required.

2 Draw your chosen pattern on paper to the same size as the table surface to use as reference, or draw directly on the table (see above). Starting from a focal point, or the edge of a colour in the pattern close to the centre of the table, start to fix the tiles in place. Unless it is ready mixed, mix the tile adhesive following the manufacturer's instructions. Dab adhesive on to the back of each tile with a small wooden spatula. Place the tiles on to the table top with a slight twisting motion to ensure adhesion, slowly building the pattern from the starting point. Work carefully, making sure that the spaces between the tiles are even and that the tile surfaces are level.

3 When the design is complete, leave the tile adhesive to dry completely. Then, wearing disposable rubber gloves, mix the grout and work it into the table surface with your fingers and a rubber spatula, ensuring the spaces between the tiles are filled. Before the grout is completely dry, wipe the surface with a clean cotton rag to remove grout from the tiles. When the grout is dry, again wipe vigorously with the cotton rag to remove any remaining powdered grout and to polish the table surface.

1

2

materials

Metal and wood/hardwood chairs

Rust cure and proofing paint (plus
    appropriate solvent)

Oil-based undercoat

Satin finish oil-based paint

Exterior-grade opaque oil- or water-
    based wood stain

equipment

Metal paint scraper

Coarse emery paper or cloth

Coarse wire brush

Medium-grade glasspaper

25mm (1in) paintbrush

Wire wool and white spirit

decorated chairs

Garden chairs are essential in any outdoor scheme. Whether you have the smallest town garden or the largest country estate, sitting outside is probably one of summer's great pleasures. Garden seats come in all shapes and sizes and the moulded plastic ones that proliferate in gardens today do provide robust and affordable seating, for all their somewhat dull uniformity. Old garden seats, typically made of wood with metal frames, are often recreated in rustproof cast aluminium or plastic-coated steel. Again, these are eminently practical yet do lack something of the battered charm of original chairs. Modern technology, however, has developed a number of paints and stains that will not only allow you to revive old chairs, but also make sure that they will last long into the future.

For this project we chose to decorate a set of 30-year-old iron and wooden café chairs, long past their prime and on the point of being consigned to the waste dump. The second set of modern unvarnished hardwood chairs, made in the Far East and bought locally, was stained to match a previously constructed folding garden table.

metal and wood café chairs

1 Carefully rub down any rusty metal using a metal paint scraper and course emery paper to remove any loose paint or metal. When the loose material has been removed, use a wire brush to clean the metal. (Modern rust cure and proofing paints are very effective and do not require all rust residue to be removed. However, care should be taken not to paint over wet metal or any loose or flaking material. Read and follow the manufacturer's recommendations carefully.) Treat any old painted wood in a similar manner, using medium-grade glasspaper. Make sure that all cracks are sanded down and that any loose material is removed.

2 Paint the metal parts with rust cure and proofing paint, taking care to cover all the metal so as to eliminate any subsequent water penetration to untreated metal. Leave the paint to dry fully before painting the wood with an oil-based undercoat. Leave the undercoat to dry overnight to ensure a good base for the subsequent finishing coats.

3 Paint each entire chair with two coats of a satin finish oil-based paint, allowing the first coat to dry fully before applying the second. These chairs were painted in muted shades from a proprietary "historic" collection – chairs painted in complementary yet different shades like this can look particularly effective.

hardwood chairs

1 First check that your chairs are not already varnished. Varnished chairs will require complete rubbing down to base wood to provide a satisfactory surface, or it will prove impossible to apply a durable stain finish. If your chairs have been treated with an oil finish it will be necessary to rub them down using wire wool and white spirit and to finish them with an oil-based stain. If the chairs are untreated, they may be finished with a water-based stain. Check a small, unobtrusive area first with water-based stain. If the surface rejects the stain, then it is likely that the timber has been treated with oil.

2 Paint the chairs with the appropriate opaque wood stain, ensuring all areas are covered. Leave the chairs to dry well before using.

materials

2.29m (7ft 6in) length of 230 x 25mm
  (9 x 1in) rough-sawn softwood
  timber, cut into:
    One 1.37m (4ft 6in) length [top]
    Two 460mm (1ft 6in) lengths [legs]
2.74m (9ft) length of 100 x 15mm
  (4 x ⅝in) rough-sawn softwood
  timber, cut into two lengths of 1.37m
  (4ft 6in) [side pieces]
Waterproof PVA glue
40mm (1½in) lost-head nails
Approx. 650mm (2ft 1½in) length of
  10mm (⅜in) wooden doweling

equipment

Hand saw
Hammer
Pencil
Tape measure
Electric drill
32mm (1¼in) hole cutter
10mm (⅜in) spade bit
Straight edge
Jig saw or band saw
Adjustable bevel
Protractor
Electric orbital sander or coarse-grade
  glasspaper and sanding block

cider bench

A bench is a very practical type of seating, especially if you are short of space as benches take up a lot less room than chairs. This bench is just as suitable for indoor use as it is in the garden. Based on a traditional Somerset design, similar benches can be found in farmhouse gardens and cider barns throughout England's West Country and, indeed, most of rural Britain. The "ocean drift" finish (see page 116) used on the bench is particularly suitable for this piece but, since it is not fully waterproof, the bench, as with most wooden garden furniture, should be taken indoors in winter or during very wet periods. Alternatively, the bench can be made using planed rather than rough-sawn timber and given a gloss paint or waterproof stain finish for year-round protection.

1 Start by fixing the two 1.37m (4ft 6in) lengths of 100 x 15mm (4 x ⅝in) softwood timber to the sides of the single 1.37m (4ft 6in) length of 230 x 25mm (9 x 1in) timber to make the top and sides of the bench, using waterproof PVA glue and 40mm (1½in) lost-head nails.

2 To make the bench legs, take one of the 460mm (1ft 6in) lengths of 230mm x 25mm (9 x 1in) timber and, using a pencil, mark a point halfway across the width and 175mm (7in) from one end – this end will be the bottom of the leg. Drill a hole centred on this point, using an electric drill and a 32mm (1¼in) hole cutter. Repeat with the second leg. Then measure 50mm (2in) in from each side of the plank at the bottom of each leg and use the pencil to mark these two points. Use the pencil with a straight edge to draw lines from these points to the respective

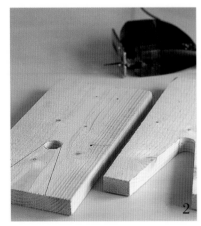

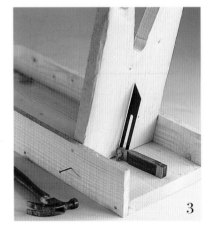

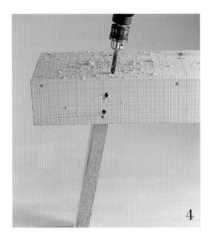

sides of the drilled holes then cut out the marked leg splays using a jig or band saw.

3 To work out the position for the legs, turn the assembled bench top upside down, measure 150mm (6in) from each end and mark with the pencil. Position the legs inside the bench top, in line with the pencil marks and against an adjustable bevel opened to approximately 75° in order to get the

correct angle for the legs. Glue the legs in position and secure carefully by hammering in two lost-head nails through the side panels and into either side of the legs.

4 Turn the bench upright to begin the process of strengthening the area where the legs join the top of the bench. Using a 10mm (⅜in) spade bit, drill two holes, approximately 32mm (1¼in) deep, through the side panel and into the side of each leg – one hole close to each lost-head nail. Then, drilling at an angle in line with the legs, drill two holes, approximately 60mm (2½in) deep, through the bench top and into the top of each leg.

5 Cut the 10mm (⅜in) doweling into eight 40mm (1½in) lengths and four lengths of 75mm (3in). Smear the shorter dowels with glue and insert them into the side holes, hammering them gently home until almost flush with the surface. Repeat the process

using the four longer lengths of doweling for the holes in the top of the bench. Saw off the ends of all the pieces of doweling flush with the surface of the wood.

6 Round off all the corners and sharp edges of the bench using an electric sander or coarse-grade glasspaper and a sanding block. To finish the bench, apply wood stain or the "ocean drift" finish (see page 116).

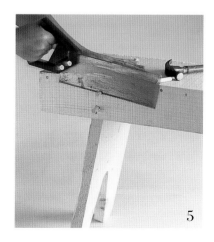

5

hammock

In the garden, the hammock, which originated in the South Americas, is perhaps one of the most powerful evocations of lazy summer days. Garden hammocks come in a bewildering variety of designs and sizes, ranging from woven nylon aberrations to fancifully tasselled and embroidered examples. The hammock shown here is made from readily available materials. The unbleached canvas used in its construction is robust and long lasting, and may be dyed or decorated in any number of imaginative ways. Rivets have been used to avoid the need to stitch heavy canvas material. If you have the skills, or the necessary equipment, however, there is no reason why the hammock should not be sewn.

Lastly, if you have difficulty in fitting the brass rings required for this project, a visit to a friendly tent or canvas awning maker might be profitable. He will have machinery designed to do this job simply and speedily.

materials

2.5m (2¾yd) length of 90cm (36in) wide medium-weight (500g/16oz) unbleached canvas

4.8 x 14mm blind rivets

M5 washers

12mm (½in) brass eye ring punch kit

1.8m (6ft) length of 25mm (1in) doweling, cut in half

8mm (⁵⁄₁₆in) staples

Two 50mm (2in) galvanized metal rings

15m (16yd) rope, cut in half

Twine or string

Two 75mm (3in) galvanized spring (lanyard) hooks

equipment

Tape measure

Pencil

Electric drill

4mm (³⁄₁₆in) drill bit

Blind rivet gun

Staple gun

Craft knife

1 Fold over 25mm (1in) at one end of the length of canvas, then fold over again to create a 75mm (3in) deep hem. On the folded hem, draw a pencil line parallel with and 12mm (½in) from the first folded edge. Holding the canvas securely to prevent the material from twisting, drill seven holes along this line, starting approximately 35mm (1½in) from one side and continuing at roughly 140mm (5½in) intervals, to finish 35mm (1½in) from the other side.

2 Secure the hem with blind rivets inserted through the drilled holes from the unfolded side of the canvas – each rivet driven through the canvas with a blind rivet gun and secured on the underside with a washer. Repeat the whole procedure at the other end of the canvas.

3 At one end of the canvas and, in a similar manner to step 1, draw a pencil line on the riveted hem parallel with and 25mm (1in) from the first folded edge. Starting at approximately 105mm (4¼in) from one side of the hem and using an eye ring punch kit, make six holes along this line at roughly 140mm (5½in) intervals for the brass rings that will hold the rope. Fit the brass rings, inserting them from the underside. Repeat the process at the other end of the canvas.

4 Feed a length of 25mm (1in) doweling through the riveted hem at each end and secure to the canvas using a staple gun. You are now ready to thread the rope through the brass rings. Lay the length of canvas on a flat surface and choose one end of the hammock to work on first. Place a galvanized metal ring approximately 800mm (2ft 7½in) from this end. Mentally number the brass rings from one to six running from one side of the hammock to the other. Tie a knot in one end of one of the lengths of rope and pass the rope from the underside of the canvas through brass ring no. 2 until it is stopped by the knot. Feed the end of the rope through the galvanized ring and then back to brass ring no. 1. Pull the rope through to the underside of the canvas then back to the galvanized ring, pulling the full length of the rope through each time – always maintaining the 800mm (2ft 7½in) distance between the hammock and the galvanized ring. Now pass the rope through brass ring no. 6 to the underside of the canvas, then again back to the galvanized ring. Next, feed the rope to brass ring no. 5, passing the rope from the top of the canvas through to the underside and then passing it up through the adjoining brass ring no. 4 to the galvanized ring. From here, pass the rope through the

top of the remaining brass ring, no. 3, to meet the knotted end of rope on the underside of brass ring no. 2. Undo the knotted end and join the two ends of rope together in one knot. Repeat the procedure at the other end of the hammock with the remaining rope and galvanized ring.

5 At each end of the hammock, make sure all the lengths of rope leading from the brass rings to the galvanized ring are even. Gather the rope beneath each galvanized ring and bind securely using twine or string.

6 Finally, fit galvanized spring hooks to the galvanized rings at each end of the hammock by which to hang it. For safety's sake make sure that your hammock is hung from secure fixings in a tree, post or wall and test it for weight before using.

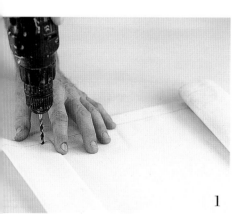

1

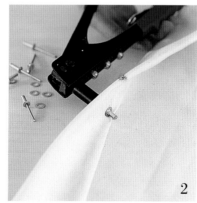

2

3

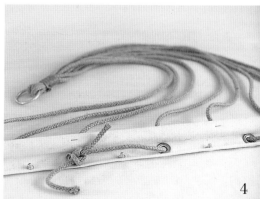

4

stencilled garden tray

Stencilling is an age-old technique, which has long been used for walls, friezes, fabrics and furniture. Over recent years it has re-emerged to become very popular. Many ready-cut stencil patterns of all kinds are available from hobby and craft shops but it is particularly satisfying and remarkably easy to cut stencils from patterns or designs of your own.

The technique can be as complex or simple as the pattern you select. The sunflower pattern chosen for this project is particularly appropriate for the garden and has been stencilled on to an old baker's tray by Susie Gradwell, who discovered the tray tucked away in a corner of her cottage garden shed.

materials

Wooden tray

Selection of matt emulsion paints

Lining paper

Cut stencil

Selection of artist's acrylic tube paints, for tinting

Exterior-grade satin acrylic or polyurethane varnish

equipment

Medium-grade glasspaper

25mm (1in) paintbrush

Low-contact masking tape

Stencil brush or 9–12mm (⅜–½in) short, flat artist's bristle brush

Kitchen paper

Paint mixing tray

Small natural sponge

If necessary, water down the paint until the desired consistency is achieved. Do not load your brush with paint; instead stencil with a dry brushwork technique, using smooth strokes and building and blending layers of paint until the desired colour has been achieved. When you are confident with the technique, start to stencil the tray and continue until the stencil is complete.

1   Begin by sanding the tray with glasspaper to provide a key for the paint. If you are using an old tray, as here, make sure it is clean of all dirt and grease. Paint the tray using two coats of matt emulsion paint in your chosen colour, allowing the paint to dry between coats. For testing stencil techniques and paint colour densities, it will be useful at this stage to paint a waste piece of lining paper in the background colour, too. Leave the tray to dry for at least 4 hours after the second coat.

2   Fix the stencil to the tray with strips of low-contact masking tape to prevent movement during stencilling. Take a stencil brush or a short, flat artist's bristle brush and, starting with the base colour of your stencilled design (generally the lightest colour), dip it lightly in your selected matt emulsion paint and wipe it with kitchen paper – this removes excess paint and prevents colour from bleeding under the stencil. Test for colour density and paint consistency on the background-painted lining paper.

3   Remove the stencil and leave the tray to dry. When dry, replace the stencil and start to apply shading and selected highlights using the same painting technique as before. A small, dry natural sponge can be used to achieve a different textured finish. Remove the stencil, carefully peeling off the masking tape, and put to one side.

4   Allow the tray to dry thoroughly. To finish the tray apply a coat of varnish, using satin finish acrylic or polyurethane varnish following the manufacturer's recommendations.

cutting your own stencil

1 If you wish to cut your own stencil, photocopy your chosen design and enlarge or decrease it to the size required for the final stencil. Trace over the pattern on to good-quality tracing paper. If your design calls for several colours, you must divide the pattern into the different colours and cut a stencil for each. To prevent tearing during use, make sure that at least 3mm (⅛in) is left between the shapes to be cut out. If you propose to produce a single colour stencil, or intend to shade and highlight the finished work by hand, you will need only one stencil.

2 Lay a sheet of acetate – the material normally used for stencils – over the tracing and cut out one or more stencils, using a sharp craft knife.

3 Alternatively, very successful stencils can be cut from heavy-duty cartridge paper, which is less expensive than acetate. Simply place a sheet of carbon paper between your tracing and a sheet of heavy cartridge paper. Draw over your pattern to transpose the design on to the cartridge paper, then cut out one or more stencils from the paper.

garden lights

A garden should be enjoyed for more than just the daylight hours. It is a good idea to install electric lighting in your garden and have its intensity controlled by a dimmer switch. Secrete lamps and spotlights in foliage and flower beds – with care and good design you can create an entrancing outdoor area that extends your living space into the garden. But, although electric lighting has its uses, the light cast by oil lamps and wax candles is far more attractive – mellow, soft and always flattering. A romantic dinner in the full glare of electric light fails to evoke a romantic mood, while muted candlelight on the other hand suits the mood perfectly. An imaginative display of lamps and candles will set the mood for any circumstance, be it a barbecue or a dinner *à deux*.

Garden flares are popular and useful, while simple and inexpensive night lights in cylinders of perforated zinc cast a fascinating mottled shadow – if placed in small gilded flowerpots the indirect light shimmers and glitters – and candles in luminously painted jam jars cast coloured light over a wide area. This project offers another possibility: the transformation of old garden tools into striking and highly individual candle holders – conversation pieces that will ornament any dining table.

materials
Timber, for tool stand
Old hollow-handled garden tool head
Builder's adhesive
Wood stain or wax (optional)
Candle (to fit tool head)

equipment
Pencil
Hand saw or drill

1 Choose soft or hardwood timber to make a stand of a sufficient size to support the tool to be used without danger of it overbalancing.

2 If using a pronged tool, such as a fork or a pitchfork, for your garden light lay the tool on the stand and mark the position of the prongs. Drill holes in the stand for each prong, to match the prong size and at an angle to ensure that when the tool is inserted, the tool head will be vertical. Put a dab of builder's adhesive in each hole and insert the tool. Leave the adhesive to dry, supporting the tool during drying if necessary.

3 If using an edged tool for a candle holder, use a saw this time to cut a slot in the stand of a size that will accept the tool (see left). Fill the

slot with adhesive and insert the tool, again making sure that the handle is vertical. Leave the adhesive to dry, supporting the tool during drying if necessary.

4 Once the builder's adhesive is dry you can stain or polish the timber stand if you like or leave it as it is.

5 Insert the candle into the tool handle. Most old tool handles can be bent open or closed as necessary to accept a candle that otherwise would not fit.

Somerset trug

This trug is a simple yet timeless design, inspired by the local wooden baskets made centuries ago in England's West Country. The original Somerset trug we made was based on one that we first saw almost 20 years ago in a local farm sale when the accumulated possessions of generations of a local farming family were sold at auction by the retiring farmer. Apparently used for collecting mushrooms from the fields in early autumn mornings, for collecting free-range eggs from their chickens or for taking hot lunchtime food to the workmen cutting hay or collecting apples from the cider-apple orchards, the basket had been used for a myriad of purposes. Battered and scuffed, with only a trace of its original paint, it was ignored by the mass of eager buyers snapping up harrows and bill hooks, cheese presses and old horse-drawn carts.

Our design for the Somerset trug became the first in a range of over 40 wooden accessories and furniture we make and sell to buyers throughout Britain and abroad. Still one of our favourite designs, we use these trugs for collecting cuttings or flowers from the garden. Indoors they make ideal storage for old magazines in the study or vegetables in the kitchen but they really come into their own as striking table displays, overflowing with fresh flowers or potted plants, or filled with candles for an alfresco evening meal.

The design for this trug can easily be adapted to produce a deep-sided tray, perfect for bringing afternoon tea into the garden – to be enjoyed sheltered from the hot sun under the shade of a tree. Simple instructions for making the tray follow the Somerset trug project.

1

materials

1.95m (6ft 4½in) length of 95 x 8mm (3¾in x ⁵⁄₁₆in) planed softwood timber, cut into:
    Two 380mm (1ft 3in) lengths [sides]
    Two 250mm (9¾in) lengths [ends]
    Two 345mm (1ft 1½in) lengths [base]
540mm (1ft 9½in) length of 30 x 8mm (1⅛ x ⁵⁄₁₆in) planed softwood timber, cut into two 270mm (10¾in) lengths [handle supports]
Waterproof PVA glue
25mm (1in) panel pins
15mm (⅝in) panel pins
335mm (1ft 1½in) length of 25mm (1in) hardwood doweling or a broom handle

equipment

Pencil
Tape measure
Straight edge
Hand saw
Hammer
Try square
Electric planer or hand plane
Electric orbital sander or medium-grade glasspaper and sanding block

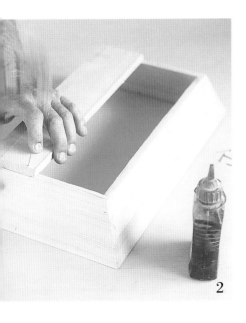

2

3

4

1 Take the two 380mm (1ft 3in) lengths of timber for the side pieces and shape them, as follows, so as to create the correct angles for the splayed sides of the trug. On one of the long sides of each board, make pencil marks 30mm (1¼in) from each end. Using a pencil and a straight edge, join these marks to the corners on the opposite long side of the rectangle and cut along the lines with a hand saw. Follow the same process with the two 250mm (9¾in) lengths to create correctly splayed end pieces. Apply glue to the end grain of the side pieces and secure the end pieces to the side pieces with 25mm (1in) panel pins.

2 Use a try square to check that the corners of the assembled carcase are square, then apply glue to the bottom edges of the piece and secure it

to the two 345mm (13½in) base pieces with 25mm (1in) panel pins. Leave the glue to dry before planing and sanding any excess wood from the base edges so that the base finishes flush with the angle of the sides and ends of the trug. When planing the ends of the trug across the grain, be sure to work away from the corners in order to prevent the wood splitting.

3 Take the two lengths of 30 x 8mm (1⅛ x ⁵⁄₁₆in) planed softwood timber for the trug's handle supports. Use glasspaper to round off the top of one end of each length. Smear the bottom 75mm (3in) of one side of each support with glue and fix to the centre of each side of the trug on the outside, using 15mm (⅝in) panel pins. Make sure that the supports are at right-angles to the sides of the trug.

4 Place 25mm (1in) hardwood doweling or a broom handle against the top of the handle supports and mark the angle of splay to allow the handle to fit securely within the supports, approximately 6mm (¼in) from the top of the supports. Cut the handle to the marks and glue and fix it in position, using three 25mm (1in) panel pins at each end. Leave the glue to set before undertaking any further work to your completed trug (see over).

finishing your trug

These trugs and trays look particularly attractive given a distressed paint finish (see page 117). While their flat surfaces invite treatment as a "canvas" for stencilling and decoupage, their classic simplicity of shape also allows for the effective use of single-colour paint and stain treatment. If left outside for protracted periods, the trugs and trays should be treated with preservative wood stain or exterior-grade varnish.

adapting the project to make a garden tray

1 It is a simple matter to adapt this project to make an attractive and practical garden tray. You will not require the handle or handle supports and should replace the two 250mm (9¾in) lengths of 95 x 8mm (3¾in x ⁵⁄₁₆in) planed softwood timber for the end pieces with 120 x 8mm (4¾ x ⁵⁄₁₆in) timber. The additional equipment required will be an electric drill and a 32mm (1¼in) hole cutter bit and a jig saw with a wood-cutting blade.

2 Cut a curve in these larger end pieces. The curve starts 95mm (3¾in) from the base at each end of the end pieces curving up to reach a height of 120mm (4¾in) in the middle. To make the handle cut-outs, drill two holes in each end piece, with their centres 45mm (1¾in) down from the curved edge and 65mm (2½in) apart. Draw pencil lines in line with the curved edge to join the top and bottom of the holes together. Cut along the lines with jig saw to make the handle cut-outs and sand the rough edges smooth with glasspaper. Shape and assemble the components just as for the trug to complete your tray.

wind and weather

The weather and the passing of the seasons affect our lives in numerous obvious and less obvious ways. It is easy to forget how important wind and weather were to our forefathers: a good season promised plenty and a wet season or a late wind could ruin a harvest and meant that people risked starvation.

Our moods, too, are affected by the weather. Crisp winter days invite brisk energetic walks in parks or in the countryside; dank chill days provide an excuse for lazing by a log fire, high winds tire and exhaust us while continuous rain can cause depression. It is human nature to enjoy sunlight and warmth and we all welcome the coming of spring, bringing with it a lifting of the spirits and renewed vitality.

Go back in time and tell the hour from a sundial made to precise calculations for the location in which you live; watch your weather vane move in the breeze, shelter from the sun under a home-made awning and take pleasure from a wind chime's restful melodies.

It would be difficult to write on the subject of weather without a mention of global warming and the apparent effects it is having on our lives and climate. Our weather is changing and we are told by the experts that these changes will become even more pronounced with the passage of time. We must plan for, and adapt to, different climates and environment, and while opinions differ over its effects and the time scale given for the changes, we are told that European summers will be hotter and winters less cold. Britain's island climate will become more pronounced, the summers more like those of continental Europe and the winters wet and stormy; while El Niño's periodic appearances in the Pacific will become more frequent with disturbing effects on weather patterns throughout the Americas and perhaps worldwide. We have all experienced the beginnings of these changes and must prepare for their effects.

above *A "crinkle crankle" wall surrounding an Edwardian kitchen garden, designed for shelter and to give trained plants maximum exposure to the sun*

right *A collection of plants and objects on a marble slab in a sheltered garden*

below left *A vertical sundial on the wall of a West Country cottage. Installed by mathematician, Eric Garland, the sundial tells local time and is 11 minutes slow of Greenwich Mean Time (GMT)*

below *A sundial gnomon cast in bronze and set on a stone plinth in a sculptor's riverside garden*

Wind and the weather dictate how we use our gardens. In clement weather we make more use of our outdoor space; when a cold wind buffets and rain beats against the window panes, we prefer to batten down the hatches and stay indoors. Hedges, walls and fences are usually erected to establish a boundary or as a screen to block out ugly buildings or undesirable neighbours. As well as providing privacy, they can also offer shade or shelter from the wind. An imaginative city dweller might erect high screens around a terrace to act as a clever and practical windbreak and create a micro-climate for rich and exotic plants in pots and troughs.

A small enclosure, be it an awning or a growing arbour, will provide protection from the elements and enhance the warmth from even the weakest winter sun. The relentless heat of the high summer sun suggests the need for shade. If none exists, provide a parasol, or build and plant a latticed bower, shrouded in leafy vines or climbing honeysuckle. Sunlight filtered through foliage casts dappled, dancing shadows across walls and surfaces of paving, slate, pebble or stone, all of which can look quite different with changes in the light and weather – rain bringing out any variations in colour to full effect. Of course, you can take advantage of the sun, too, by building your own feature sundial.

left *A bronze galleon sails ever onward into the wind. This charming weather vane is fitted to the slate roof of a summer house*

right *A simple metal weather vane surmounted by a Welsh dragon.*

below left *Hunt stables often feature weather vanes in the form of a fox in flight like this one, or a pack of hounds in full cry*

below right *A weather vane in the design of a galloping horse surmounts an ancient farm building*

The slow deliberate movement of a weather vane reacting to the wind, the fresh scent of grass recently rained upon, the notes of a wind chime hanging from a branch or the bell-like sounds from chimes set on slender wands of steel, the buzz of insects, the gentle rustle of tall grasses in a soft breeze or the sounds of running water – all have a therapeutic and calming effect on stressed souls.

Weather vanes are most often seen on ecclesiastical buildings or country houses, and often quite whimsical ones are frequently a feature of old farm buildings, sometimes depicting the owner's profession or farming speciality or perhaps merely a whim of the builder or mason. The weather vane on buildings owned by a cattle farmer may depict a cow, for example, while that of an arable farmer may display a carthorse or a workman wielding a scythe.

The tradition has survived to this day: training stables may feature a galloping horse, a house owned by a keen sailor may have a racing yacht with billowing sails or a motoring enthusiast may display a vintage car. Many examples of more simple weather vanes merely showing the points of the compass are quite common. Early examples of weather vanes, fashioned from iron or carved in wood, have become collectors' pieces and some make fascinating mantelpiece ornaments – a reminder of an earlier, less complicated time.

This weather vane has been designed to be used as an ornament or it may be adapted for outdoor use. Look through old books and photographs, find a pattern or image that appeals to you – anything from a crowing cockerel to a contemplative owl – and use it to create your own weather vane.

materials

Approx. 760 x 320mm (30 x 12½in) piece of 20mm (⅞in) thick laminated softwood board or exterior-grade block board or plywood

Black matt emulsion or oil-based paint plus oil-based primer and undercoat

125mm (5in) length of 15mm (⅝in) copper piping

Waterproof PVA glue

Soft- or hardwood timber, for stand

100mm (4in) length of 12mm (½in) galvanized metal bolt or rod, to fit inside 15mm (⅝in) copper piping

Ball bearing, to fit inside 15mm (⅝in) copper piping

Acrylic or polyurethane exterior varnish

equipment

Pencil or felt-tip pen

Tape measure

Jig saw, coping or fret saw

Electric drill

15mm (⅝in) spade drill bit

32mm (1¼in) hole cutter (optional)

12mm (½in) spade drill bit, or size to fit bolt or metal rod

Medium-grade glasspaper

25mm (1in) paintbrush

weather vane

1 Choose a design for your weather vane. Enlarge or reduce it to fit your piece of board, allowing 50mm (2in) from the base of the design to the bottom edge of the board. Draw a feathered arrow outline on the board, the top of the shaft to be 50mm (2in) from the bottom of the board. Then draw the outline of your design, the front facing towards the arrow head. Ensure that the centre of the design is approximately 25mm (1in)

towards the rear from the centre of the length of board. Draw the support for the weather vane, approximately 32mm (1¼in) wide, under the centre of the board.

2 Carefully cut out the design and the arrow using a jig saw with a fine blade or a coping or fret saw. To cut out any enclosed areas, drill holes in the board first, using a 15mm (⅝in) spade drill bit or a 32mm (1¼in) hole

cutter, which will allow the insertion of the jig saw blade.

3 Sand smooth the cut and rough edges of the board. Paint the weather vane with either oil-based primer, undercoat and top coat (for use outside) or two coats of black emulsion paint (for interior display), allowing the paint to dry between coats. When the paint is completely dry, use a drill and a 15mm (⅝in) spade bit to cut a hole in

the base of the weather vane support, approximately 32mm (1¼in) deep. Be very precise, making sure that you drill accurately and that the spade bit does not emerge from the sides of the timber. Apply glue to the drilled hole in the timber and insert the 125mm (5in) length of copper piping into the hole.

4 If you wish to display your weather vane on a stand you will require a piece of hardwood or

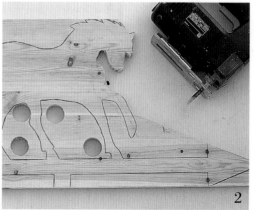

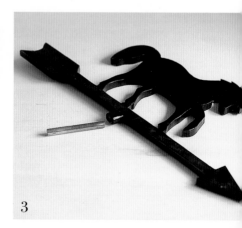

softwood timber of sufficient size to support it securely. The weather vane will need to be supported on a galvanized or other corrosion-proof metal bolt or rod, at least 100mm (4in) long and of a size (approximately 12mm/½in) to fit loosely inside the 15mm (⅝in) copper piping in the weather vane support. Drill a hole through the timber stand of a size to take the bolt or rod. Apply glue to the hole and insert the bolt or rod in position, ensuring it is vertical. Leave to dry. When the glue is dry, place the ball bearing inside the copper piping and fit this over the bolt or rod, allowing the weather vane to revolve freely.

5 If you wish to display your weather vane outside, give it at least three coats of exterior-grade varnish to protect it from the weather. To fix in position, either secure the bolt or rod in the desired location using sand and cement, or fit it to a piece of timber as above and nail or screw it securely to the wall or roof.

wind chimes

equipment

Hacksaw

Tape measure

Jig saw

Metal cutting blade

Electric drill

5mm (³⁄₁₆in) high-speed
  metal drill bit

Metal rasp file

Medium-grade emery
  paper or cloth

Pliers

Hearing is one of the most important yet least considered of the senses. Sounds can entrance or infuriate. The inconsiderate use of machinery, loud music or even boisterous voices often lead to disputes between neighbours. Quiet is a coveted requisite of modern urban life and many gardens are designed specifically to create areas of peace and respite. Sound is part of everyday life but the secret of achieving tranquillity is to create sounds that you will find calming and restful.

The sound of running water appeals to almost everyone, the song and chatter of wild birds and the muted buzz of insect life are part of summer's allure, while a strategically placed wind chime, situated where it will catch a balmy summer breeze, can provide both a focal point and musical tones welcome in any garden.

This project shows how to create two different wind chimes. Do not be limited by the materials we chose for these chimes – use what is available to you or what you think will make a pleasing note. For the second wind chime we used marlin spikes for the chimes. Marlin spikes are available from most good ship's chandler's shops and rope-makers and are still used for binding wire rope. Made of heavy cast steel, they are ideal as wind chimes as they make a particularly attractive musical note when struck. Marlin spikes are heavy and this wind chime would be most effective in windy conditions rather than light breezes.

materials

Wind chime 1

Approx. 175 x 125mm (7 x 5in) light-
  gauge galvanized steel sheet

Six 32mm (1¼in) spring (lanyard) hooks

Two 25mm (1in) split key rings

Three large and 2 small bells or chimes

300mm (1ft) length of 15mm (⅝in)
  copper piping

300mm (1ft) length of 12mm (½in) link
  plated steel chain

1.6m (1¾yd) jewellery chain, cut into
  4 equal lengths

Metal "S" hook

wind chime 1

1 Cut a triangle out of the sheet of steel using a jig saw with a fine metal cutting blade. Using a 5mm (³⁄₁₆in) high-speed metal drill bit, drill two holes 6mm (¼in) from the edge of the metal – one in the apex of the triangle and one centred along the opposite side. Smooth all the sharp edges using a metal rasp file and emery paper or cloth.

2 Insert a 32mm (1¼in) spring (lanyard) hook through the eye of one small bell and hang it from the hole in the apex of the triangle. Insert a split key ring through the second drilled hole. Drill holes through the ends of the copper piping, 12mm (½in) from each end. Insert the key ring already fitted on the steel triangle through the holes in one end of the

copper piping and a second split key ring through the holes in the other end. Fit the link plated steel chain to the second key ring and attach a spring hook to the free end of the chain.

3 Clip the remaining spring hooks and bells to one end of each of the four lengths of jewellery chain. Gather the loose ends of chain and fix them to the spring hook already attached to the plated steel chain. Insert the metal "S" hook into the spring hook and hang the wind chime from a hook or nail in a breezy location where it can swing freely.

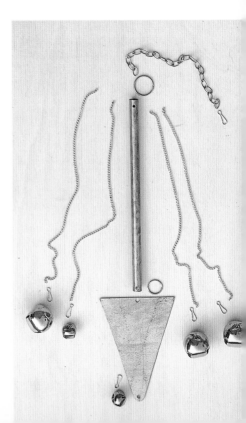

wind chime 2

1 Using a jig saw and metal cutting blade, cut two circles from the light-gauge galvanized steel – one about 175mm (7in) in diameter, the second 115mm (4⅝in) in diameter. In both circles drill two 5mm (³⁄₁₆in) holes opposite each other, approximately 6mm (¼in) from the edge of the metal. Drill four further holes in the larger steel circle: two either side of one of the existing holes, positioning them at 25mm (1in) intervals and, again, 6mm (¼in) in from the edge of the circle. Smooth all sharp edges with a metal rasp file and emery paper or cloth.

2 Insert a split key ring in each of the two holes in the smaller steel circle and the spring hooks in all six holes in the larger circle. Join the two circles together passing the split key ring in the smaller circle through the spring hook inserted in the single hole in the larger circle.

3 Feed the remaining split key rings through the holes in the marlin spikes. Take the five lengths of plated steel chain and fix one end of each to the split key rings inserted in the marlin spikes and the other ends to the spring hooks in the larger steel circle. Feed one end of the remaining length of plated steel chain through the split key ring in the smaller circle, insert the metal "S" hook in the chain and hang the wind chime in a windy location.

materials

Wind chime 2
Approx. 300 x 175mm (12 x 7in) light-
  gauge galvanized steel sheet
Seven 25mm (1in) split key rings
Six 32mm (1¼in) spring (lanyard) hooks
Five 200mm (8in) steel marlin spikes
1.75m (5ft 9in) length of 12mm (½in)
  link plated steel chain, cut into:
    5 lengths of 300mm (12in)
    1 length of 250mm (9in)
Metal "S" hook

horizontal sundial

The earliest known sundial was discovered in Egypt and dates from some 5,000 years ago. Before the advent of mechanical clocks, primitive water clocks and sundials were the only means of accurately recording time. Although many European churches show evidence of early vertical sundials on their walls, the need for measuring time was largely unimportant for agrarian people. Dawn and dusk dictated the passing of their days and there was little need for hours or minutes.

This sundial is made from slate but various other materials including concrete are acceptable. Once positioned, your sundial should not be moved, so the weight of materials used in its construction is relatively unimportant. Although simple sundials can be purchased, they will not be accurate unless made for your locality. Sundials tell local time and must be adjusted to compensate for mean or zone times. The time depicted by your sundial will differ from zone time by its longitude east or west of the zone's meridian. To make a properly working sundial, designed for a particular situation, a little work with paper and pencil is required first.

materials
Tracing paper
Approx. 500 x 500mm (20 x 20in)
    square of 25mm (1in) thick slate slab
Right-angled triangle of slate, approx.
    18mm (¾in) thick x 350mm (14in)
    base length, for the gnomon – the
    height of the slate will be dictated by
    your location
Two-part exterior stone adhesive
Metal Roman numerals I to XII
    including 2 no. VIs (optional)
Tile adhesive

equipment
Pencil and large sheet of paper
Ruler
Pair of compasses
Protractor
Carbon paper
Masking tape
Angle grinder
Thin stone-cutting disc
Safety goggles
Dust mask
Straight edge

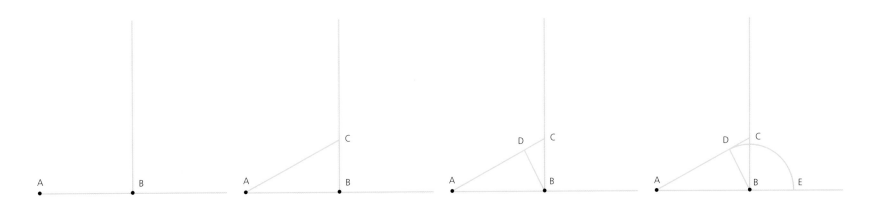

the mathematics

1 Draw a horizontal line towards the bottom of the paper. In the centre of the line draw a vertical line perpendicular to the horizontal line. Mark the left point of the horizontal line as **A** and point where the lines intersect as **B**. The larger the piece of paper you use, the easier it will be to draw accurate angles and the more accurate your sundial will be.

2 Draw a line from point **A** at an angle that is equal to the latitude of the proposed location of your sundial (see a map of your area), to intersect the vertical line at point **C**. This angle will be the angle for the construction of your gnomon, the triangular piece which casts the shadow on the completed sundial.

3 Draw a line from point **B** that is perpendicular to the line **AC**, joining **AC** at point **D**.

4 Measure the distance from **B** to **D**. Mark this same distance on the horizontal line to the right of **B** to make point **E**. Centre the compasses on point **B** and join points **D** and **E** with a curved line.

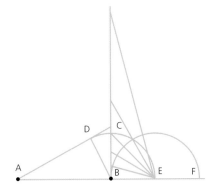

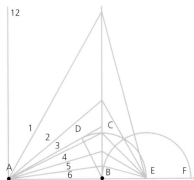

5 Centre the pair of compasses on point **E** and draw a semi-circle from point **B** to point **F**. Using a protractor, divide the left half of the semi-circle into five 15° sections – accuracy is most important here. Draw lines with pencil and ruler from point **E** to intersect the vertical line through the 15° marks.

6 Connect the points where the lines intersect your vertical line to point **A**. You have now created the afternoon hours for your sundial. Draw a vertical line from point **A** to represent your noon line.

7 To create your morning hour lines, you need to recreate lines, identical to the afternoon ones, to the left of your noon line. The easiest way to achieve this is to make a tracing of the afternoon lines on a sheet of tracing paper. Turn the sheet over so that the lines are repeated to the left of the vertical line at point **A**. Go over

the tracing in pencil in order to transpose the markings on to your original plan. Congratulations! You have now created the plan for the face of your sundial.

making your sundial

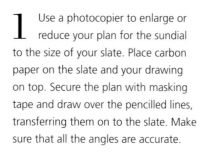

1 Use a photocopier to enlarge or reduce your plan for the sundial to the size of your slate. Place carbon paper on the slate and your drawing on top. Secure the plan with masking tape and draw over the pencilled lines, transferring them on to the slate. Make sure that all the angles are accurate.

2 Carefully cut the marked lines in the slate using an angle grinder and a thin-gauge stone-cutting disc. Use a metal straight edge if you like to help you cut accurate lines.

3 Cut the triangle of 18mm (¾in) slate using the angle grinder with one 90° angle and one angle as calculated in Step 2 on page 43. If you do not have an angle grinder ask a stone mason or floor tiler to cut the triangle for you with a large disc diamond cutter.

4 Place the triangle of slate on the 12 noon line of the sundial base with the calculated angle positioned on the horizontal base line of the grid and fix it in place with two-part stone adhesive. If you have chosen to use Roman numerals on your sundial, secure them with tile adhesive at the ends of the hour lines, as shown in the last diagram on page 43.

5 Your sundial should be situated in an open position and not overshadowed by any trees or buildings. If you live in the northern hemisphere the gnomon (12 noon line) of your sundial must point towards true north. Remember that true north is not the same as magnetic north so a compass should not be used to orientate the sundial. You can locate true north in one of three ways:

i) Use an accurate large-scale survey plan of your location with longitude marked on it to locate north.

ii) Choose a clear night and locate the North (Pole) star. Set the gnomon of your sundial to point at the star.

iii) On a clear sunny day, place a vertical rod on the place you wish to locate your sundial. When the shadow thrown by this rod is at its shortest (in the middle of the day) the shadow is pointing at true north.

6 When you have located true north secure your sundial in position on the top of a wall or a plinth, using sand and cement or builder's adhesive.

IMPORTANT SAFETY NOTE – The disc will create considerable dust, so be sure to wear safety goggles or other eye protection and use a dust mask.

garden awning

In colder climes, summer with its sun and warmth is eagerly anticipated and welcome when it comes, but we are being increasingly warned of the dangers of over exposure to the sun's rays. A garden without shade is an incomplete garden. There are numerous and attractive garden umbrellas available, but should you be a little more adventurous and wish to ornament your garden with an individual shaded structure that does not require years of growing, is portable and easily stored when not in use, why not attempt this garden awning project? Adjust the size to suit your own garden or the awning's envisaged use. Any material can be used. We used some heavy antique French linen sheets salvaged from a *brocante* (bric-a-brac shop) in Normandy, draped over the frame and secured with tape and large safety pins, plus braid and antique curtain tassels for effect. Alternatively you can make a purpose-made cover.

1 On one end of each of the four 2m (6ft 6in) legs, mark a line 50mm (2in) from the end around all sides of the timber, using a tape measure, try square and pencil. Cut around the line on each piece with a panel saw, taking care to cut no more than 4mm (³⁄₁₆in) deep. Use a chisel to pare away the excess timber, leaving the ends of the legs to fit tightly within the lengths of square-section steel.

2 Glue and fit the four lengths of square-section steel to the chiselled ends of timber (to make the top of the legs. Using a 10mm (³⁄₈in) drill bit, drill a hole 32mm (1¼in) deep into the end grain at these reinforced ends. Apply glue to the holes in the timber and insert the steel rods. Allow to dry.

3 Drill a 6mm (¼in) hole through both ends of each rear and side strut, 20mm (⅞in) from the end. To make the crossed support piece for the rear of the frame, drill a 6mm (¼in) hole through the centre of both rear struts and join them together with an M5 bolt, washer and nut.

4 Lay two of the legs on a flat surface, parallel to each other, about 1m (3ft 3in) apart. Drill a 6mm (¼in) hole approximately 125mm (5in) from the steel end of each leg. Lay the crossed and joined rear struts on top and temporarily secure to the legs with bolts inserted through the holes in the ends of the struts and in the top of the legs. Mark the point where the lower ends of the struts fall and drill 6mm (¼in) holes in each lower leg. To conceal the bolt heads, countersink the holes in the legs, approximately 12mm (½in) deep, using a 12mm (½in) drill bit.

5 Disassemble the crossover struts from the rear legs. Lay one of the rear legs on a flat surface, the drilled holes uppermost and 760mm (2ft 6in) away from a front leg. Measure and mark a point halfway down the rear leg and drill a 6mm (¼in) hole through it at right-angles to the previous holes, countersinking as before. Insert a bolt to connect the leg to one end of two side struts. Join the other ends of the side struts to the front leg with M5 bolts, washers and nuts. Repeat, joining the other rear leg to the other front leg and the two remaining side struts. Join the two sides of the frame together with the crossover rear struts, securing with M5 bolts, washers and nuts.

6 Stand the frame upright with the steel-capped timber at the top. Take the remaining struts for the top of the frame and drill 12mm (½in) holes in the ends of each, 20mm (⅞in) from each end. Place the struts for the front, back and sides over the protruding steel rods, and then fit the top diagonal strut across the top of the frame.

7 Drape your fabric over the frame. For a purpose-made cover, you will need two pieces of fabric about 2.20m (2yd 15in) long by 90cm (35½in) wide for the sides, and one piece about 3.65m (4yd) long by 140cm (51in) wide for the top and back. Press a double 2.5cm (1in) hem to the wrong side of all edges and then machine-stitch. At one end of each side piece insert a brass eye ring in each corner, using an eye punch kit. If desired, sew a fringe to one end of the top and back piece. Place this long piece over the frame, leaving the front hanging to form a pelmet. Mark the position of the four steel rods on the fabric and then insert four brass eye rings. Fit the side pieces to the frame first by placing the brass rings over the protruding steel rods. Then place the top and back piece in position.

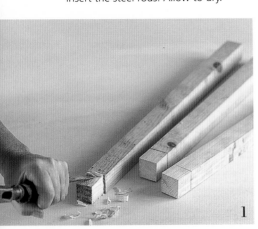

1

2

3

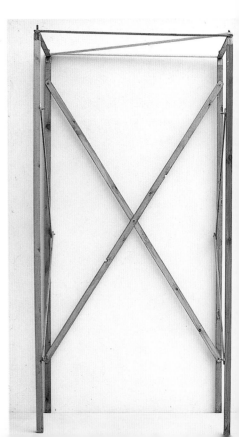

materials

Four 2m (6ft 6in) lengths of 32 x 32mm
 (1¼ x 1¼in) planed softwood timber
 [legs]
40 x 10mm (1½ x ⅜in) planed softwood
 timber, as follows:
 Two 1.86m (6ft 1in) lengths
 [rear struts]
 Four 1m (3ft 3in) lengths
 [side struts]
 Two 1.015m (3ft 4in) lengths
 [top front and back struts]
 Two 775mm (2ft 6½in) lengths
 [top side struts]
 One 1.27m (4ft 2in) length
 [top cross member]
Four 50mm (2in) lengths of 30mm
 (1⅛in) square-section steel
Four 75mm (3in) lengths of 10mm (⅜in)
 steel rod
Waterproof PVA glue
Eleven 60mm (2½in) M5 bolts, washers
 and nuts
Fabric (throws, curtains, sheeting), to
 drape or for a purpose-made cover
 (see step 7) plus sewing cotton and
 12mm (½in) brass eye ring punch kit

equipment

Tape measure
Try square
Pencil
Panel saw
25mm (1in) chisel
Hammer
Electric drill
10mm (⅜in) drill bit
12mm (½in) drill bit
6mm (¼in) drill bit

birds and wildlife

The almost indiscriminate use of chemical based fertilisers, pesticides and herbicide in the search
for ever higher crop yields has culminated in a dramatic loss of wildlife habitat and therefore
indigenous wildlife, throughout much of the developed world.

The time has come for us to attempt to do what we can to help preserve and encourage the
wildlife that gives so many of us so much enjoyment and helps keep the balance of the natural
world. Town and country gardens provide important wildlife habitats, home to both resident and
seasonal visiting birds, animals and insect life. We can have a significant effect on the wildlife
that uses our gardens simply through the provision of food, water and places for birds and animals
to find shelter and breed. In this chapter we show you how to make a bird nesting box, construct a
bird bath, build a bird feeding table and assemble a bat box, small but important contributions
you can make to entice day and nocturnal wild visitors to your garden.

Gardens attract birds and wildlife. Ever since man began to cultivate land there must have been trouble from competing animals, insects and birds – not to mention weeds. The enjoyment and advantages that wildlife brings you and your garden far outweigh any depredation they may cause. A colourful border attracts butterflies and even if weeds do proliferate they give a home to many different varieties of insect as well as shrews, voles and other small mammals. Birds will nest and take shelter in trees, hedgerows and even in a well-manicured shrubbery. Water is a natural habitat for dragonflies and even a modest garden pond made from an old cast-iron bath sunk into the ground and cleverly disguised with ground cover, stones and ferns will give a home to newts and frogs, as well as providing drinking water for many species of birds in dry weather conditions.

A growing awareness and concern for the risks to wildlife from the use of so many chemicals in horticulture and farming has led to a renewed interest in replacing these with biodegradable and natural substances whenever possible. The most obvious effect of the overuse of pesticides and herbicides has been the loss or reduction in numbers of once common species of birds and insects. These have been deprived of their natural foods, killed by chemicals or driven away through loss of habitat – the sad demise of so many summer butterflies being probably the most apparent case. Encourage animals and birds to visit your garden by providing food all year round and, if there is no natural water, install a bird bath.

left *An unusual bird table made from an old candelabra. Note the larger dish on the right, made specially for a visiting "pet" pigeon*

above *A garden pond constructed from an old enamel bath sunk into the ground, surrounded by natural stone and planted with ferns*

above *A pump head fitted inside a ceramic pot trickles water on to pebbles in a small home-made garden water feature*

below *A wooden bird nesting box with side netting to encourage the growth of climbing plants and provide space for insect hibernation*

Some insects are a garden pest and others are beneficial, but we owe it to our environment to help provide all wild creatures with safe havens in our gardens. There has been much discussion about the "wild" garden: fallen trees, rampaging couch grass and bindweed, brambles rambling and clambering to bring their reward as far as deer, rabbits, hares, birds of prey, weasels, foxes and badgers, together with any number of insects, are concerned. As has been said, however, "wild gardening is certainly not entirely work free" – a thought worth pondering if you are not prepared to battle with nature.

Gardens today provide an important wildlife habitat and many wild birds, animals and insects live in and around our homes. While the mud nests of house martins under the eaves are a familiar sight, there are other birds and bats, too, that live and nest in our roof spaces. The construction of modern houses, however, and the recent trend towards efficient home insulation have eliminated many of these sites. Increasingly, wild animals and birds suffer from a lack of suitable habitat, so the provision of well-constructed animal houses, bird nesting boxes, feeding tables and water baths in both town and country gardens not only provide an important resource for wildlife, but also attract wildlife to our gardens and give us a great deal of pleasure. Don't forget that wildlife – particularly birds, bats and hedgehogs – as well as being an attractive feature of your garden, also fulfils a very useful function as efficient natural controllers of many insect pests.

right *A nesting box "condo" with apartments for three nesting birds – a pretty item although probably not very practical if the birds are territorial*

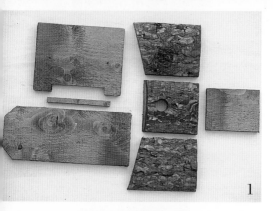

1

2

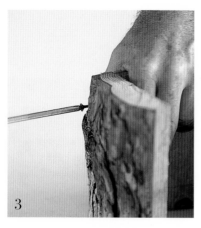

3

bird nesting box

Nesting boxes come in all shapes and sizes but this one is a simple closed box, which has been designed to attract a wide variety of garden birds. A 25mm (1in) hole will attract smaller birds, while a 32mm (1¼in) one will appeal to larger hole nesting birds. The box can be modified to suit birds that prefer an open nesting site by eliminating the hole and cutting away 50mm (2in) from the top of the front panel. It is a misconception that nesting boxes should be fitted with a perch, since most birds will cling to the hole itself or to the rough wood surrounding it. Perches can in fact provide access for unwelcome predators to attack the nest.

The box has been constructed from rough-sawn softwood timber and offcut timber, complete with its original bark, obtained from a local sawmill. This barked timber is the largely unwanted side product of many sawmills and can often be secured at little or no cost. The box can as easily be made entirely from rough-sawn softwood timber, planed timber or waterproof plywood. Cleanliness is important with all bird boxes as disease can easily spread from accumulated dirt. This nesting box has been constructed with a removable top, secured with rust-proof brass screws, which allows it to be cleaned at the end of each nesting season.

4

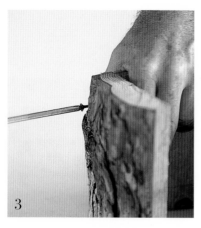

5

1 Firstly, cut out and shape the components as in picture 1. Take the back piece and cut off 25mm (1in) from the corners of one short end. Saw the barked timber into three sections: one front piece 165mm (6½in) long and two side pieces 200mm (8in) long. Angle the top edge of each side piece – sloping from 165mm (6½in) at the front to 200mm (8in) at the back. Take the roof piece and on one long side cut out a strip of timber measuring 150 x 20mm (6 x ¾in), 40mm (1½in) from either end, using a saw and chisel.

2 Cut the end grain on the top edge of the front section at an approximately 15° angle to match the sloping angle of the side pieces and to make sure that the nesting box will be water and wind tight. Drill a 25mm (1in) or 32mm (1¼in) hole in the middle of the front piece, 110mm (4¼in) from the base. Stain the pieces with preservative wood stain making sure that all cut edges are saturated.

3 Insert the front piece between the two side pieces. Pre-drill two screw holes each side, then glue and screw the front in place, using 40mm (1½in) cross-head screws and making sure that the 15° angle on the top edge of the front is flush with the sloping angle of the sides. Drive the screws into the solid timber so that the heads are concealed within the bark.

4 Fit, glue and screw the back piece within the sides of the box in exactly the same manner, allowing for its straight bottom edge to be flush with the base of the nesting box.

5 Fit the 150 x 125mm (6 x 5in) base piece of rough-sawn timber inside the nesting box, flush against the front piece and butting up to the bottom edge of the back piece. Pre-drill screw holes then again glue and screw into place, using two 40mm (1½in) cross-head screws on each side. Fit the roof piece to the top of the box,

placing the cut-out over the back piece. Pre-drill one hole in the centre of each side of the roof and, without using glue, screw the roof to the box, using two 40mm (1½in) no. 8 brass screws. To make a waterproof seal between the back and the roof, fit the piece of 12 x 12mm (½ x ½in) softwood on top of the roof using three 25mm (1in) cross-head screws, or secure 50mm (2in) rubber seal in place with 12mm (½in) steel tacks.

6 To fix your nesting box, use nails or screws to fit it securely in its selected site. Nesting boxes should be sited in a sheltered position, at least 2m (6ft 6in) above the ground on a wall or tree and away from any overhanging branches, which might allow cats or other predators to raid the nest. Ideally, a nesting box should be hung facing north or east, away from prevailing winds and the heat of the midday sun.

materials

355mm (1ft 2in) length of 150 x 12mm (6 x ½in) rough-sawn softwood timber [back]

Approx. 565mm (1ft 10½in) offcut timber complete with bark, trimmed to 150mm (6in) wide [front and sides]

230mm (9in) length of 175 x 12mm (7 x ½in) rough-sawn softwood timber [roof]

Approx. 150mm (6in) length of 125 x 12mm (5 x ½in) rough-sawn softwood timber [base]

Medium-brown water-based non-toxic preservative wood stain

Waterproof PVA glue

40mm (1½in) cross-head screws

Two 40mm (1½in) no. 8 round-head solid brass screws

150mm (6in) length of 12 x 12mm (½ x ½in) softwood plus three 25mm (1in) cross-head screws, or 150mm (6in) length of 50mm (2in) rubber seal plus 12mm (½in) steel tacks

Nails or screws, for positioning the box

equipment

Tape measure

Pencil

Hand saw

Try square

25mm (1in) chisel

Electric drill

25mm (1in) or 32mm (1¼in) hole cutter

2mm (¹⁄₁₆in) drill bit

25mm (1in) paintbrush

Cross-head screwdriver

bat box

Bats are fascinating but regrettably often much-maligned animals. Their swooping flight at dusk and early evening as they chase insects, is a constantly mesmerizing sight. Silent to most ears, their high-pitched squeaking, used to echo-locate their prey in flight, can in fact be heard by some adults with particularly sensitive hearing, and many small children. In several countries bats are under threat as their habitat decreases and many species are protected.

While bird nesting boxes are a familiar sight, the erection of a more unusual bat box in your garden will not only give it an added attraction, but also provide a very useful home for an endangered animal.

This bat box has been constructed from rough-sawn timber. It could be made from planed timber or plywood but the rear and inside faces of the box must be constructed from rough surfaced or grooved timber to allow bats to cling to it.

materials
Approx. 1.2m (4ft) of 150 x 12mm
   (6 x ½in) rough-sawn timber, cut into:
   One 355mm (14in) length [back]
   One 165mm (6½in) length [front]
   One 175mm (7in) length [roof]
   Two 200mm (8in) lengths [sides]
   One piece measuring approx.
   100 x 125mm (4 x 5in) [base]
Medium-brown water-based non-toxic
   preservative wood stain
Waterproof PVA glue
32mm (1¼in) annular ring nails
Nails or screws, for positioning the box

equipment
Tape measure
Pencil
Hand saw
25mm (1in) paintbrush
Electric drill
2mm (1/16in) drill bit
Try square
Hammer

1 Shape the top of the long back piece by sawing off 25mm (1in) from the corners of one short side. Next, shape the angled sides of the box. First mark out then saw one short edge of each side piece so that the sides of the box, when vertical, slope down from a height of 200mm (8in) at the back to 165mm (6½in) at the front. Next, shape the front of the box by cutting across the end grain of what will be the top edge at roughly a 15° angle, to match the angle of the side pieces and to make sure that the box will be water and wind tight. Repeat this on the end grain of one short side of the 150 x 175mm (6 x 7in) piece of timber for the roof, again so that it will

match the sloping angle of the side pieces and also fit neatly against the back piece. Stain all of the pieces of rough-sawn softwood with preservative making sure that all the edges are well saturated.

2 To assemble the box, start by fixing the front on to the side pieces, ensuring the approximately 15° angle at the top of the front is flush with the sloping angle of the sides. Use a try square to check that the corners are square and pre-drill all the nail holes to minimize the chances of the wood splitting. Glue and then nail the pieces in place, using two nails on each side of the front piece.

3 Next, fix the back piece on to the side pieces, leaving 90mm (3⅝in) of the unshaped bottom of the back piece protruding beneath the base of the box. Rest the base of the box on the edge of your work surface for support and fit the roof of the box with its angled edge flush against the back piece of the box. Finally, insert the base inside the box and glue and nail in place, leaving a 50mm (2in) entry opening at the rear of the box.

4 Nail or screw the box to a wall or tree. Like bird nesting boxes, bat boxes should be placed out of reach of predators and away from direct sunlight or prevailing winds.

bird table

materials

Rough-sawn softwood timber:

2.4m (7ft 10in) length of 175 x 12mm
(7 x ½in), cut into:
 Four 410mm (1ft 4in) lengths [base
 and roof support frame]
 Two approx. 400mm (1ft 3in) lengths
 [roof ends]

2.21m (7ft 3in) length of 40 x 12mm
(1½ x ½in), cut into:
 Four 230mm (9in) lengths [uprights]
 Two approx. 340mm (1ft 1½in) lengths
 Two approx. 300mm (12in) lengths

6.2m (20ft 6in) length of 25 x 12mm
(1 x ½in), cut into:
 Eight 350mm (1ft 2in) lengths
 [edging for base and roof support
 frame]
 Four 230mm (9in) lengths [uprights]
 Two 255mm (10in) lengths [roof end
 supports]
 Four 200mm (8in) lengths [roofing
 strips supports]
 Four lengths of approx. 290mm
 (11½in) [barge boards]

760mm (2ft 6in) length of 100 x 12mm
(4 x ½in) [decorative frieze]

2.76m (8ft 6in) length of 100 x 6mm
(4 x ¼in), cut into 6 lengths of
approx. 460mm (1ft 5in) [roofing
strips]

Waterproof PVA glue

25mm (1in) panel pins

Four 40mm (1½in) brass- or zinc-plated
 steel screw eyes

Four 915mm (3ft) lengths of 10mm
 (⅜in) ramin doweling

Eight 40mm (1½in) brass- or zinc-plated
 steel cup hooks

65mm (2½in) galvanized metal hook

Water-based non-toxic preservative
 wood stain

equipment

Hammer
Electric drill
32mm (1¼in) hole cutter
3mm (⅛in) drill bit
Try square
Tape measure
Pencil
Hand saw
25mm (1in) paintbrush

The best food for wild birds is that on which they normally feed: the seeds and berries provided by indigenous plants and the insects that live on them. Additional food will provide a useful supplement, however, and in hard times can be essential to birds' survival. It is most important that if you do decide to provide food, you do so all year round as the birds can come to depend on it. The food you provide should be varied so as to attract a wide variety of birdlife, and should always be clean, as should the bird table. Bread, mixed seeds and fat are excellent food for birds while peanuts, which are always welcome, should be either hung underneath the table in a mesh feeder or crushed to prevent them being fed whole to young chicks during the breeding season.

The bird table for this project has been designed to fulfil a number of important functions. It is dual-purpose in that it provides a useful nesting box in its roof. It is designed to be suspended in order to keep it out of the reach of marauding cats and it is roofed to keep food dry in wet weather and moist in hot weather. Its size should prevent it being raided by larger and often unwelcome birds, and its design ensures that it will be an attractive addition to any garden. In addition, it has a hole in the base to simplify cleaning.

This project calls for a number of different dimensions of timber. Whether you use rough-sawn timber or plywood, you will find that an electric saw table will prove particularly useful.

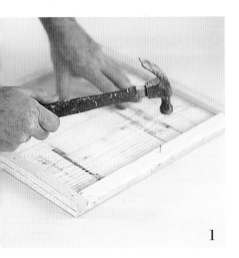

1 Make up the base of the table by gluing together, side by side, two of the 410mm (1ft 4in) lengths of timber. Secure them with four of the 350mm (1ft 2in) long edging pieces, glued and nailed with their edges flush to the edges of the base, to form a 410 x 350mm (1ft 4in x 1ft 2in) base frame. Repeat with the other two 410mm (1ft 4in) lengths of timber and the remaining four pieces of edging to make the roof support frame. Drill a 32mm (1¼in) drainage hole 40mm (1½in) away from one of the base frame's corners.

2 Now join the two frames together at each corner, the flat unframed sides facing each other, with corner supports constructed from the four 230mm (9in) lengths of 40 x 12mm

(1½ x ½in) and the four 230mm (9in) lengths of 25 x 12mm (1 x ½in) timber, using glue and 25mm (1in) panel pins. Fit the 25mm (1in) wide upright pieces on the long sides of the frames, flush with the corners, and overlap the 12mm (½in) width with the 40mm (1½in) wide upright pieces pinned and glued to the short sides of the frames so that the face of each corner support is roughly 40mm (1½in) wide. Use a try square to check that the corners are square.

3 Fix a 255mm (10in) length of 25 x 12mm (1 x ½in) timber on top of the edging on the two short sides of the roof frame (the one without the drainage hole) with glue and 25mm (1in) panel pins. Measure between the newly fixed corner

supports (approximately 360mm (1ft 2in) for the long sides and 300mm (12in) for the ends of the frames) and cut 40 x 12mm (1½ x ½in) timber to fit. Fix to the four sides of the base frame, using glue and panel pins to conceal the edging.

4 To make the decorative frieze, take the 760mm (2ft 6in) length of 100 x 12mm (4 x ½in) timber and draw a line lengthways along the centre of the timber. Mark points along this line at 50mm (2in) intervals starting approximately 25mm (1in) from one end. Drill holes through the timber using a 32mm (1¼in) hole cutter.

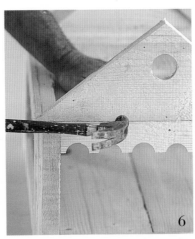

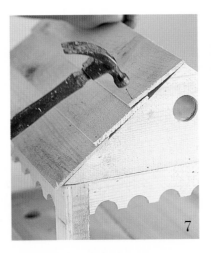

5 Saw along the line through the holes to make two 760 x 50mm (2ft 6in x 2in) strips. Cut each strip into two (making four lengths) to fit between the corner uprights, flush with the roof frame. Secure the decorative frieze with glue and panel pins.

6 Cut two triangles approximately 400mm (15in) long by 150mm (6in) high from 175 x 12mm (7 x ½in) timber to make the two roof ends. Drill a 32mm (1¼in) hole in one piece 65mm (2½in) from the apex of the triangle. Fix two 200mm (8in) lengths of 25 x 12mm (1 x ½in) timber to the sloping sides of each triangle, flush with the edges and mitred at the top of the triangle to fit the apex – these will be inside each roof end to provide support for the roofing strips. Fix the roof ends to the roof frame, gluing and nailing them on to the 255mm (10in) roof end supports previously fitted.

7 Measure the length of the bird table between the roof ends (approximately 460mm (1ft 5in)) and fit

three lengths of 100 x 6mm (4 x ¼in) timber or plywood for the roofing each side of the roof, fixing them to the roofing supports with glue and panel pins. Starting at the bottom, fix the first strip to overhang the bird table edge by approximately 12mm (½in); overlap the remaining two roofing strips to finish flush with the apex of the roof. Repeat on the other pitch of the roof, making the final strip overlap the top strip on the first side for a tightly sealed roof, which will keep out the rain.

8 To conceal the gaps where the roof strips overlap, fix two barge boards (approximately 290mm/11½in long) each end, made from 25 x 12mm (1 x ½in) timber and mitred at the apex to fit. Secure these to the roof ends with glue and panel pins. Cut two decorative finials from offcuts of timber and use to cover the joint in the barge boards at the apex at each end of the roof, securing them with glue and panel pins. Use your imagination to decide on a pattern for your finials to give your bird table an individual look.

9 Lastly, insert four 40mm (1½in) brass- or zinc-plated screw eyes into the corners of the bird table roof. Take the four lengths of ramin doweling and drill a 3mm (⅛in) hole in the end grain of each. Dab glue on to the eight cup hooks and insert one in each end of the lengths of doweling. Allow the glue to dry.

10 To complete your bird table, paint it and the doweling rods with a preservative wood stain. Allow to dry and then attach each piece of doweling to the bird table by placing the cup hooks through the screw eyes fixed to the roof.

11 Finally, screw a 65mm (2½in) galvanized metal hook into a suitable branch or overhang, where the bird table will be well out of the way of any cats or other predators. Hang the bird table from the cup hooks, fed through the galvanized metal hook. Chain may be used instead to hang the bird table but doweling does help the stability.

materials

75 x 25mm (3 x 1in) planed softwood
 timber

50 x 25mm (2 x 1in) planed softwood
 timber

Approx. 200 x 200mm (8 x 8in) square
 of 20mm (¾in) thick planed softwood
 or exterior plywood (base piece)

Approx. 400 x 400mm (1ft 4in x 1ft
 4in) square of 20mm (¾in) thick
 planed and laminated softwood or
 exterior plywood (base piece)

Plastic rimmed seed tray or similar
 rectangular shallow watertight
 container (maximum 75mm (3in)
 deep)

Approx. 63mm (2½in) architrave
 moulding

*NB The amount of timber and
architrave moulding needed will be
determined by the size of the tray*

40mm (1½in) zinc-plated cross-head
 screws

Waterproof PVA glue

Wood filler

Softwood newel post

Four 32mm (1¼in) softwood or beech
 knobs

Exterior-grade, non-toxic wood
 preservative and coloured wood stain

equipment

Tape measure

Pencil

Hand saw

Electric drill

3mm (⅛in) drill bit

Cross-head screwdriver

Mitre saw

Medium-grade glasspaper

Try square

25mm (1in) paintbrush

bird bath

Birds need water just as much as we do. In hot weather when natural water sources have dried up this is particularly necessary, but it is just as important in cold conditions when ice may prevent birds from drinking. All birds enjoy bathing and while some use dust baths to help rid themselves of parasites, they bathe in water with evident enjoyment.

It is important that a bird bath should be kept filled with fresh water and is cleaned regularly to prevent the spread of parasites and disease. There are many designs of bird baths to choose from but we have chosen one that will be an attractive addition to a garden or patio, can be cleaned simply and may easily be adapted to serve as a feeding table. It has the additional advantage of being portable, although it could be turned into a fixed structure by eliminating the base construction. The lengths of timber required for the project will depend on the size of the plastic watertight container you are using. For the bird bath base, you may find it preferable to use exterior-grade plywood since it resists bending, is easily worked, very robust and most importantly, is more readily available and far less costly than solid or laminated softwood.

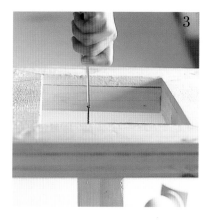

1 Start by making a frame for the plastic container. Mitre four lengths of the 75 x 25mm (3 x 1in) planed softwood timber to form a frame for your plastic container and align them on the work surface. Cut four pieces of the 50 x 25mm (2 x 1in) timber to the same outside dimensions as the mitred frame and place on top. Pre-drill holes for the 40mm (1½in) cross-head screws then glue and screw both frames together, using the butted joints of the second frame to secure the mitred corners of the first frame.

2 If the depth of your plastic container is 50mm (2in) or less, use 50 x 25mm (2 x 1in) timber, if it is more, use 75mm x 25mm (3 x 1in) timber and cut it into four lengths to fit inside the second frame within the rebate formed by the two frames. Pre-drill the screw holes then glue and screw these lengths of timber into place. When the glue is dry, measure the width of the rectangular opening and cut a length of 75 x 25mm (3 x 1in) timber to make a cross member to fit across the centre of the rectangle just inside the opening and flush with the frame to form the support for the plastic container. Again, pre-drill the screw holes before gluing and screwing the cross member in place and check that the timber is level. Cut the architrave into the required lengths with a mitre saw and glue and screw the pieces (pre-drilling the holes first) to the outside of the frame in order to hide the unsightly joints. Fill any screw holes with wood filler, sanding it smooth when dry.

3 Cut the decorative top off the newel post, using a try square and pencil to ensure an accurate cut.

Place the frame on top of the post, pre-drill screw holes through the cross member, then glue and screw in place.

4 Fit the smaller base piece, approximately 200mm² (8sq in) and cut from planed softwood or exterior plywood, to the base of the newel post with glue and screws (pre-drilling the holes first) and the larger piece, approximately 400mm² (16sq in) and cut from planed and laminated softwood or exterior plywood, underneath. Measure and mark a point approximately 50mm (2in) from each corner of the larger base piece. Pre-drill screw holes, then glue and screw a 32mm (1¼in) knob at each point, underneath the base piece, screwing them from what will be the top of the base piece when the bird bath is upright. These knobs are important as they will keep the base structure off the ground and help it resist wood rot.

5 Treat the bird bath with exterior-grade wood preservative and paint or finish with coloured wood stain or preservative. Make sure that all of the end grain is thoroughly saturated with preservative.

creative containers

Containers planted with flowers or shrubs can be used for an instant effect in a new garden or to rejuvenate a neglected area. Terracotta chimney pots in different sizes, oak whisky barrels sliced in half, old metal fire buckets and tin tubs, watering cans, milk churns and stone, earthenware and porcelain sinks have all at some time been recycled for use in container gardening.

Look around you and see what might be transformed into a useful container for growing plants. You may choose to make a display of cacti or a table centrepiece for outdoor entertaining, or find a new lease of life for a redundant vessel by filling it to overflowing with flowers and ferns. In this chapter we show you how to transform an orange box into a container for herbs or as an attractive table decoration, convert a polystyrene fish box into a "stone" planter and make and decorate a number of more traditional wooden garden planters. "Perfect pots" provides a selection of simple but effective ideas for decorating terracotta and plastic plant pots.

left A terracotta container fixed high on a trellis support and planted with ivy

below A "forgotten" stoneware urn heavily encrusted with lichen growth, half-hidden in a bed in a cottage garden

Containers can be used in all sizes of garden, from the largest area to the very smallest rooftop retreat. Portable planters are particularly useful for creating areas of interest, which can be changed around with the passing of the seasons and as different plants reach their peak. Create small focal areas in the garden by using gravel, pebbles and different coloured stones (paint stones, if you wish, for a striking effect) to set off displays of large-leafed plants in grouped containers. Wooden containers made to hold pots of herbs, or orange boxes transformed into table-top containers for outdoor dining are easy to make and rewarding in their effect. Secrete a hanging pot high among the leaves of a climbing creeper or create small planted displays of pots in areas to be discovered and rediscovered as you walk around the hidden areas of your garden.

Giant antique terracotta pots from the Mediterranean or Mexico, once used for storing olives, wine or water, make interesting focal points; big objects in small gardens can in fact give an illusion of space. Terracotta literally means "cooked earth" and these hand-made vessels, some as large as two or three metres in height, have developed a unique character of shape, size and colour through generations of use. However, they are not always easy to find, and are becoming increasingly expensive.

above *A selection of hand-thrown
and decorated modern terracotta pots
and containers, featuring traditional
"Long Toms" in the background and
moulded and surface-decorated pots in
the foreground*

right *A simple water feature made
from an old oak whisky barrel*

right *This old stone trough that has been filled with coloured pebbles makes an attractive garden ornament.*

left & below *Collection of late 19th- and early 20th-century clay pots, seed trays and a rhubarb forcer, discoloured, chipped and battered with use*

Garden centres sell a wide range of modern terracotta but, although reasonably priced, such containers tend to be machine made and mass produced and lack the charm of older pots. Modern terracotta can be successfully aged and distressed, however, using natural yogurt (see "Ageing Terracotta", page 122). Certainly, do not dismiss all modern terracotta as there are some exquisite examples of plain and decorated pots and planters made by local craftsmen. Search out these potters and you will be fascinated by some of their contemporary wares and the designs still being made in traditional style. Your acquisitions will give you years of pleasure, as well as supporting local craftspeople.

Within a garden, a good view can be emphasized or attention can be diverted from a plain wall with the careful positioning of terracotta, reconstituted stone or even concrete urns and pots, which eventually become so encrusted with lichen that they appear to be antique.

For the urban gardener with only a window box, a postage stamp-sized patch or rooftop garden, pottering about arranging and rearranging or replanting the various containers can give hours of pleasure and respite from the pace of a busy city life. When it comes to the choice of plants, it is preferable to restrict the range and colour scheme, as this will make a far greater impact in a small space than attempting to include a bit of everything.

material

Old 100mm (4in) terracotta flowerpot

Old terracotta ridge tile

Zinc-plated or galvanized 40mm (1½in)
   M5 bolt, nut and 2 washers

equipment

Waste timber or board

Tape measure

Pencil

Electric drill

5mm (³⁄₁₆in) masonry drill bit

Spanner to fit M5 nut

terracotta wall planter

Wall planters overflowing with trailing geraniums or other drought-resistant plants are a feature of Mediterranean houses and gardens – the bright colours provide a striking contrast with the stark whites of sun-drenched buildings. The simple hand-made clay tiles and pots found throughout much of southern Europe make particularly appropriate planters but this project can be easily adapted using materials available to you. Let your imagination run free and take inspiration from a search around a building reclamation yard, which will reveal a cornucopia of different tiles that can be adapted to make a variety of unusual wall planters.

Choose a pot with a drainage hole in its base. If not, you will need to drill holes in the base before you begin the project to allow for adequate drainage.

1   2

1 Place your flowerpot on a piece of waste timber or board and make a mark with a pencil at a point on the inside of the pot approximately 25mm (1in) from the rim. Using a drill and masonry bit, drill a 5mm (³⁄₁₆in) hole through the pot from the inside. Do not use the drill's hammer action and drill with care in order to minimize the chances of cracking the terracotta. Place the ridge tile with the outer curved surface down on a sheet of waste timber or heavy card. Place the flowerpot in the tile – with the drilled hole in the middle of the rebate of the tile and the bottom of the pot approximately 25mm (1in) above what will be the bottom edge of the tile. (Many ridge tiles narrow towards one end: the wider end should be the top of your wall planter and the narrower end the base.) Use a pencil to mark the position of the newly drilled hole in the pot on to the tile. Remove the flowerpot and carefully drill a 5mm (³⁄₁₆in) hole through the tile where marked.

2 Place a washer on the 40mm (1½in) M5 bolt and push the bolt from the back of tile through the drilled holes in both the tile and the pot to join them together. Place a second washer on the protruding bolt and secure with a nut, finger tightening it only. If there are no other existing holes in the tile suitable for hanging the completed planter, drill a 5mm (³⁄₁₆in) hole in the rebate about 50mm (2in) from the top edge of the tile. The wall planter may be hung from a wall on a nail or hook from this second hole.

3 Fill the flowerpot with potting compound or compost and a suitable plant. Always keep the plant adequately watered. Fast-growing plants in small and medium-sized flowerpots will soon dry out in hot weather.

patio planter

It is tempting to think of planters as being appropriate only for small or city gardens. However, large planters set on either side of a door are always attractive, while smaller planters, perhaps painted or stained to match the colour of your house, are versatile additions to any driveway, garage area or patio. Filled with flowers, foliage, shrubs or even small trees, planters can camouflage an eyesore, act as a focal point, and give added height, colour and texture to any area of ground.

They can be almost any size or shape, made of innumerable materials and finished in any number of ways. We originally designed this planter for box-tree topiary but were so pleased with it that we made four more and have placed them, crammed with foliaged plants, around the courtyard of our old barn workshops. Adapt the size of your planter to suit the type of plant it will contain. Very few plants will thrive in small containers that restrict root growth. Plants in small containers are also susceptible to drought in summer and frost in winter.

You can fill your planter with soil, but using a container inside your planter will help protect the wood against rot and extend its life considerably. The planter here was designed to take a square plastic container inside. It is far simpler to make your planter fit an existing pot or container rather than to find a inner container that will fit perfectly after you have made your planter.

1 Place two of the upright pieces parallel to each other on a flat surface, the outside edges 395mm (15½in) apart. Mark a point 25mm (1in) from the bottom of each piece and place one short side piece horizontally across the two uprights with its bottom edge on the pencil marks and its ends flush with the outside edges of the uprights. Using a 4mm (³⁄₁₆in) drill bit, drill through the side piece at both ends, drilling approximately 6mm (¼in) deep into the uprights. Glue and secure the pieces with coach screws. Before tightening with a spanner, use a try square to check the corners are square. Next, place one long side piece across the uprights, butting it up to the already fixed short side piece, ensuring the long piece overlaps the uprights equally at both ends, by about 12mm (½in). Drill and secure with coach screws as before. Fix seven further alternate short and long side pieces across the uprights to reach the end of the uprights. A total of nine side pieces make up each completely assembled side section.

2 Repeat this step, using the remaining two uprights and a further nine side pieces, again securing them with glue and coach screws. Then begin to assemble the planter by placing the two completed side sections opposite each other. Join them with the remaining 18 side pieces, alternately using long and short side pieces so as to match them with those on the completed side sections and create flush corners. Fix the pieces as before with glue and coach screws and leave 25mm (1in) long legs exposed.

3 Stand the planter on its legs and use a try square to check that the corners are square. Measure the distance between the uprights. Cut and mitre four lengths of 65 x 18mm (2½ x ¾in) timber to this distance to make a capping that will cover the exposed ends of the uprights and the edges of the side pieces. Leave approximately 12mm (½in) to overhang the sides of the planter. Fix the capping in place with a generous amount of waterproof glue and 40mm (1½in) annulated ring nails.

4 Measure and mark the depth of the container or pot you intend to use inside the planter. Fix two 370mm (1ft 2½in) supports inside the planter opposite each other, using glue and 25mm (1in) galvanized cross-head screws, approximately 40mm (1½in) lower than the depth of the container to be used. When the glue is dry, place the six remaining 370mm (1ft 2½in) lengths of timber across the supports and fix with glue and more screws to provide a floor for the planter and keep the structure rigid. Paint the planter with at least two coats of preservative wood stain, making sure that all the end grain is well saturated.

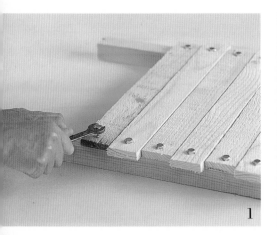
1

2

3

materials

Rough-sawn softwood timber:

Four 480mm (1ft 7in) lengths of 40 x
40mm (1½ x 1½in) [uprights]

Approx. 18m (60ft) length of 50 x
12mm (2 x ½in), cut into:

    Eighteen 395mm (1ft 3½in) lengths
[short side pieces]

    Eighteen 420mm (1ft 4½in) lengths
[long side pieces]

    Eight 370mm (1ft 2½in) lengths
[supports and floor]

Approx. 1.93m (6ft 4in) length of
65 x 18mm (2½ x ¾in), cut into 4
lengths of approx. 480mm (1ft 7in)
[capping]

Waterproof PVA glue

Seventy-two 30mm (1¼in) long 5mm
(³⁄₁₆in) square-head galvanized steel
coach screws

40mm (1½in) annulated ring nails

25mm (1in) galvanized cross-head
screws

Preservative wood stain

Plastic pot or container

equipment

Tape measure

Pencil

Electric drill

4mm (³⁄₁₆in) drill bit

Spanner

Try square

Hammer

Cross-head screwdriver

25mm (1in) paintbrush

materials

Rough-sawn softwood timber:

2.29m (7ft 6in) length of 230 x 12mm
  (9 x ½in) timber or exterior-grade
  plywood, cut into:
    Two 815mm (2ft 8in) lengths
    [box sides]
    Two 330mm (1ft 1in) lengths
    [box ends]

2.42m (7ft 11in) length of 18 x 18mm
  (¾ x ¾in) timber, cut into:
    Four 230mm (9in) lengths
    [end battens]
    Two 755mm (2ft 5½in) lengths
    [side battens]

Approx. 16.5m (54ft) length of 50 x
  12mm (2 x ½in) timber or exterior-
  grade plywood, cut into:
    Four 240mm (9½in) lengths, mitred at
    45° [corner braces]
    Thirty-eight 280mm (11in) lengths
    [cladding]
    Eight 320mm lengths (12¾in) [legs]
    Six 330mm (1ft 1in) lengths [floor]

Waterproof PVA glue

25mm (1in) panel pins

Preservative wood stain

equipment

Hand saw

Tape measure

Pencil

Hammer

Try square

Mitre saw

25mm (1in) paintbrush

window box/planter

Container displays can be used in any outdoor space. The rectangular shape of this planter is particularly suitable for use where space is limited or plants are to be trained up a wall. This planter is free-standing but may easily be adjusted for use as a window box – simply trim the legs to fit the slope of your windowsill.

The dimensions of the planter were dictated by its need to fit existing containers and can easily be adjusted to suit different-sized containers or pots. Rough-sawn softwood timber is not essential – planed timber can be used for a more sophisticated planter which can be gloss painted if preferrred. Alternatively, try using offcut timber, complete with bark, or insert tiles or slate in simple frames mounted on the side pieces (see right). If frames or straight-edged cladding are used, it is advisable to add a mitred flat frame on the top for protection and an attractive finish. It is not necessary to clad all the sides if the planter is to be used as a window box or positioned where not all faces will be on view.

1 Place the two 815mm (2ft 8in) side pieces on a flat surface. Measure and draw a line along the 230mm (9in) width, 12mm (½in) from each end on both pieces. Apply glue to one long edge on the four 230mm (9in) end battens and then stick and nail two of these to each side piece inside the pencil lines. Glue and nail a side batten on to each side piece, fitting it between the end battens already in place. Make sure that the outer edges of each side batten and side piece are flush. Place the ends of the planter against the side

pieces, butting them against the end battens. Fix with glue and panel pins.

2 Place the planter upside down so that the side battens are uppermost. Check the corners with a try square then fit the four mitred corner braces across the corners of the box, using glue and panel pins .

3 Next make the picket posts. Using a mitre saw set at 45°, cut a 90° apex on each of the 38 lengths of cladding and the eight leg pieces.

4 To fit the cladding, turn the planter on one side with the side battens and corner braces nearest you. Starting at one end of the side piece, fix a leg piece with glue and panel pins, ensuring that its outside edge is flush with the end of the planter and leaving about 70mm (2¾in) protruding below the base of the box. Proceed around the planter, securing the cladding and checking that it is fitted uniformly with approximately 25mm (1in) protruding below the base of the box. At the corners, the leg pieces on the ends of

the planter should overlap the outer edges of those on the side pieces.

5 Lastly, secure the six 330mm (1ft 1in) lengths of timber for the floor of the planter on top of the side battens with glue and panel pins. Paint the planter with preservative wood stain, making sure that all end grain is well saturated. Two contrasting stain colours were used for the planter pictured. When the preservative is completely dry, fill the planter with potted flowers, plants or shrubs.

fish box planter

materials

Polystyrene fish box

Short length of 25mm (1in) plastic pipe
or broom handle

25mm (1in) wire netting, sufficient to
cover the inside and outside walls
of the box

One part each of cement, sand, coarse
grit and peat (or similar fibrous plant
material), sufficient to cover the
inside and outside walls of the box to
a thickness of about 25mm (1in)

equipment

Sharp knife

Pliers or wire cutters

Shovel and old board, for mixing
cement

Trowel or float

Soft brush

Solid stone planters are attractive and they weather readily. They are also extremely heavy, increasingly difficult to find and today command frighteningly high prices. There has been a trend to convert old china sinks into "stone" planters but this demand and the recent fashion for reintroducing them into modern kitchens has largely exhausted an already diminishing resource. Mock stone planters, like their original forebears, also suffer from the disadvantage of being particularly heavy and fragile. The planter shown here is a modern equivalent and yet, as its name implies, is made from a polystyrene fish box. It has all the advantages of a traditional stone planter yet weighs only a fraction of the original.

You can accelerate the ageing process and encourage an attractive patina on these planters by treating them as you would new terracotta (see Ageing Terracotta, page 122). Ron Mathews, who made this planter and has made many different sized examples for his exquisite Somerset garden, is in the habit of surreptitiously pouring coffee grounds, the remnants of his afternoon tea and any number of other unmentionable substances on to his planters to encourage the growth of colourful mosses and lichens!

Fish today tends to be shipped in lidded polystyrene boxes that keep the contents well insulated, while enjoying the additional advantages of being both lightweight and cheap to manufacture. A fishmonger or seafood wholesaler should be happy to let you have one of these rectangular boxes.

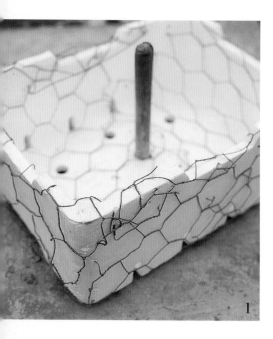

1 Cut off any extraneous moulding on the polystyrene box that might otherwise spoil the shape of your planter. Cut a drainage hole in the base of the box and insert the length of plastic pipe or broom handle, making sure that it protrudes approximately 25mm (1in) above the surface inside the box. Carefully mould wire netting over the whole of the box and secure it by weaving the cut ends of wire into the mesh.

2 Make a mixture of one part each of cement, sand, coarse grit and peat or other fibrous material. Add water and mix to a workable consistency. Using a trowel or float,

carefully apply the wet mixture to cover the interior and the sides of the wired box, to a thickness of about 25mm (1in). Smooth the surface and leave it to set, being careful to leave the plastic pipe or broom handle in place.

3 Before the concrete mix is fully set, brush it with a soft brush to roughen the surface and gently remove the plastic pipe or broom handle with a twisting motion to leave a drainage hole. When the concrete is completely dry, you can treat it as you would new terracotta to accelerate ageing (see Ageing Terracotta, page 122).

materials

Planed softwood timber:

Approx. 920mm (3ft) length of
140 x 10mm (5½in x ⅜in) timber,
cut into:
Two 250mm (10in) lengths [ends]
One 410mm (1ft 4in) length [base]

Approx. 820mm (2ft 8in) length of 90 x
10mm (3½ x ⅜in) timber, cut into
Two 410mm lengths (1ft 4in) [sides]

Waterproof PVA glue

25mm (1in) panel pins

420mm (1ft 4½in) length of 18mm (¾in)
doweling

Wood stain or matt emulsion paint

Dark wax or exterior-grade varnish
(optional)

equipment

Tape measure

Pencil

Straight edge

Hand saw

Coarse-grade glasspaper

Electric drill

18mm (¾in) spade bit

Hammer

25mm (1in) paintbrush

farrier's box

This is one of the most popular items in our range of products and its simplicity explains much of its appeal. It started life as a portable container for housing all the daily essentials for our daughter to groom her pony. The final design was adapted for a client to package a range of garden essentials for a Christmas promotion.

We use our farrier's boxes for any number of various purposes. In the house they make ideal containers for all the dozens of pens, pencils, erasers and coloured markers that would otherwise clutter our daughter's bedroom. They are also very useful receptacles for jottings on scraps of paper otherwise lost, miscellaneous keys and unopened mail in forbidding brown envelopes. In the garden we have one to keep safe all the various hand tools needed for pruning and planting around the house, another containing seed packets and liquid plant feeds, and a third for the smaller tools and essential bits and pieces that one always needs but can never find. The boxes also make particularly attractive containers for pots of flowering geraniums or fresh green herbs.

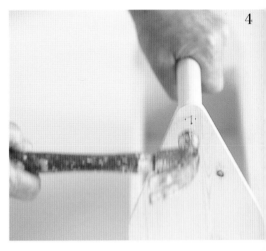

3 Apply glue to the end grain at one end of the structure, then fit an end piece to it, its drilled hole facing inward, with more panel pins.

4 Turn the structure on to its other end, apply glue to the end grain as before and into the drilled holes in the end pieces. Insert the length of doweling in the drilled hole in the fixed end piece then carefully fix the second end piece in place with 25mm (1in) panel pins. Drive two panel pins into the doweling through each end piece.

5 Complete your box with a stain finish. Alternatively, you could paint it with matt emulsion paint and when dry sand the sharp corners and edges to simulate wear, finishing with an ample coating of dark wax, rubbed well into the paint to create a fashionable distressed paint effect. If your box is to be used out of doors and subject to the weather for long periods, give it a protective finish of at least three coats of exterior-grade varnish instead of the dark wax.

herb box

This handy sized and useful box can be adjusted in size to make a small and decorative herb box – suggested overall dimensions 210 x 140 x 220mm (8¼ x 5½ x 8¾in) – ideal for planting with small culinary herbs for an unusual kitchen display. Alternatively, it is just as attractive painted in an off-white colour and packed with soaps and pretty bottles and placed in a bathroom.

1 Start by shaping the timber for the end pieces of the box. Take one rectangular end piece and find and mark the centre of the long sides. Connect these points with a lightly drawn line across the width of the timber. Next, mark the centre of one of the short sides of the rectangle. Mark two more points along this edge of the timber, at a distance of 12mm (½in) either side of the central point. Using a straight edge and solid pencil lines, join each end of the lightly drawn central line with the nearest off-centre point at

the end of the rectangle. Saw along these two solid lines then round off the corners using glasspaper. Mark and cut the other end piece in the same way. Mark a point 18mm (¾in) down from the apex of each end piece and using an 18mm (¾in) spade bit, carefully drill a hole centred on that mark, no more than 6mm (¼in) deep. Put to one side.

2 Apply glue to one long edge of each side piece and place on top of the base. Check that the structure is square; fix with 25mm (1in) panel pins.

orange box planter

It wasn't so long ago that all fruits and vegetables were supplied to the wholesaler or shop in wooden boxes (see page 65), usually branded with the supplier's name. These robust boxes were replaced by lighter wooden containers, often printed with vibrant designs and details of the country of origin of their contents. As fruits and vegetables are now shipped in from all over the world, and weight and space have become more important, these boxes are being superseded by printed cardboard.

Wooden fruit boxes can still be found, however, in a variety of sizes and shapes. We demonstrate here how to transform these fairly mundane boxes into practical containers. Use them as trays, fill them with fruit, ornamental cabbages or other attractive vegetables, perfect for a table display when eating out of doors. They are also useful for displaying a collection of herbs, as shown opposite.

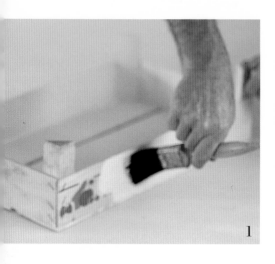

1

2

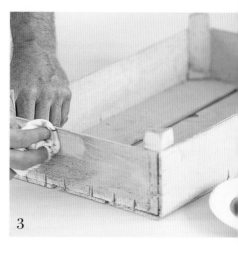

3

1 Paint a wooden orange box, inside and out with stone-coloured matt emulsion paint. Be sure to obscure any printing on the box.

2 When the paint has dried, sand off the edges and round off the corner supports to simulate the effects of age. Apply a light-coloured furniture wax, rubbing it well into the paint with a soft cotton rag. When dry, polish with a stiff brush and finish with a soft rag.

3 Now paint the entire box with antique brown liquid wax. Wipe it off immediately with an absorbent cloth, leaving a darker residue in corners and deep grain.

4 When the box is completely dry, sand it again, carefully removing wax and some paint from any edges where normal usage would show wear. Pay particular attention to soften sharp edges and corners.

5 Paint the whole box with dark oak water-based wood stain. Immediately wipe the stain off the box, before it has time to dry, with an absorbent soft cloth. The stain will be absorbed by the areas of bare wood but repelled where wax remains. If you wish and when dry, the box can be decorated with a stencil pattern. Roman numerals were stencilled on the orange boxes opposite, which adds to the "antique" style. Once the stencil

paint is dry, either finish the box with matt or silk spirit-based varnish or with a light-coloured wax applied with a soft cloth and buffed to a shine. Be careful when waxing over any stencil pattern or you may damage it. A box finished in wax may be left outside for short periods but should not be left out of doors for long periods of time.

materials

Wooden orange box
Stone-coloured matt emulsion paint
Light-coloured furniture wax
Antique brown liquid wax
Dark oak water-based wood stain
Stencil paints (optional)
Exterior-grade matt or silk
    spirit-based varnish

equipment

25mm (1in) paintbrush
Medium-grade glasspaper
Clean cotton rags
Stiff polishing brush
Cut stencil (optional)
Stencil brush (optional)

perfect pots

Flowerpots, in all their different sizes, shapes and colours, are an integral part of any garden decoration scheme. If you are buying new clay pots and live in an area that is subject to frosts, be sure to buy pots that are guaranteed frostproof. It is a little frustrating having to repot a favourite plant that has been exposed to the elements after the pot has been shattered by frost!

New terracotta has its charm, but old pots are infinitely more attractive. Clay mellows and changes colour and texture with age, and the surface weathered by wind, rain and changing temperatures attracts a variety of moulds and lichens, which over time add more and varied tones to the mysterious diversity of the clay's natural colour.

You are lucky if you already own a selection of old clay pots; if not, start searching for them, since your garden, roof terrace or patio will be enhanced by a collection of large and small antique pots. Victorian gardeners were privileged to have such a diversity of terracotta available to them – although they would doubtless have welcomed the labour-saving properties of the lightweight modern plastic pot! If you visit a specialist horticultural antique shop or an old working garden, you may see a range of the antique terracotta that was available to gardeners of old – from tall and heavy rhubarb-forcing pots and elegant 'Long Toms' to small seed trays – all hand-made and often with quite whimsical surface decoration. Old pots often bear the accidental thumb prints of their original makers, long since dead, and frequently the stamp of some obscure local pottery, a constant source of intrigue and speculation. Terracotta is fragile and if you find or already own early examples, use them with care.

Tricks of the trade can allow you to speed up the process of nature's natural ageing (see Ageing Terracotta, page 122) and a few simple techniques can transform the most brash of machine-produced modern pots into subtle yet practical collectable containers.

Experiment with colours and finishes. The following pages illustrate a number of different approaches to decorating both clay and plastic pots, and a range of materials that you may find useful. No technique is immutable and materials can be adapted, interchanged or replaced, according to what is available to you or the result you wish to achieve.

single-colour painted pots

Pastel colours and muted period shades were chosen for this project. Use your own imagination to paint pots in whatever colours take your fancy, but remember that grouped pots look best if there is some commonality of colour or tone.

1 Place your hand inside the flowerpot and paint the outside carefully with one or two coats of matt emulsion paint in a colour of your choice. Use the paint sparingly and try to avoid leaving brush marks. When the paint is fully dry – at least 3 hours after the application of the last coat – carefully sand around the rim and the base of the flowerpot with fine glasspaper or emery paper to create the look of natural wear.

2 There are various alternatives for finishing the pot. For pastel-coloured pots or lighter shades, varnish the pot, inside and out, using at least two coats of varnish, according to the manufacturer's recommendation. Allow to dry between coats and leave the pot for at least 24 hours to allow the varnish to harden before planting. For darker or muted colours, paint the outside of the pot with antique pine liquid wax. Leave it for only a couple of minutes before wiping off with a cotton rag, leaving residue in grooves and indentations to simulate an aged appearance. When the wax is dry, polish with a dry cotton rag.

4 You can leave the pot unvarnished and, over time, the unprotected emulsion paint will weather to reveal the colours of the underlying natural terracotta. However, do not allow the the painted surface to come into contact with the soil as it will stain.

materials
Terracotta flowerpots
Selection of matt emulsion paints
Exterior-grade matt varnish (optional)
Antique pine liquid wax (optional)

equipment
25mm (1in) paintbrush
Fine-grade glasspaper or emery paper
Clean cotton rags

1

2

spatter finish plastic flowerpot

There are two basic approaches to spatter painting. The first uses a stiff brush, generally trimmed to half its normal length. A finger or blade is drawn across the brush, previously dipped in watery paint, and a fine spatter of paint is directed on to the piece to be painted. This technique is used for simulating a number of exotic stones including granite and porphyry and greater detail can be found in books on paint finishes.

We demonstrate here the second method, which is more simple for the novice painter and better suited to garden decoration. It's also a lot more fun! The technique is purely decorative and lends itself to use in many areas of the garden and on many different pieces. The method is particularly messy and it is strongly recommended that you wear old clothes and undertake the technique in a work area which has been extensively protected or where mess is not important.

materials

Large plastic flowerpot
White oil-based primer
Charcoal grey matt emulsion paint
Selection of different coloured matt
   emulsion and/or artist's acrylic
   tube paints
Exterior-grade matt or satin varnish

equipment

Medium-grade glasspaper
25mm (1in) paintbrush
Waste timber or board, for use as a
   plinth
Painting cloth or considerable quantity
   of paper or board to mask work area
Protective clothing
Selection of small and medium-sized
   stiff paintbrushes
Wooden stick, approx. 300 x 25 x
   25mm (12 x 1 x 1in)

1 Take a large plastic flowerpot (a 250mm (10in) pot was used here), and roughen its surface with glasspaper to provide a key for the paint. Paint the outside of the pot and the top 75mm (3in) inside the pot with an oil-based white primer. When it is fully dry, paint the pot liberally with the grey matt emulsion paint, using a dabbing motion with the tip of the brush in order to give the surface a stippled texture. Allow to dry.

2 Place your pot on a plinth just above waist height on your workbench. To allow you to move the pot through 180° without needing to touch it, the plinth should be placed on a board. Remember, spatter painting is great fun and it gives a finish that is a little different but it is extremely messy and it is advisable to screen your work area with paper, board or sheeting so that excess paint will not cover the entire working area!

3 Practise the basic technique (see opposite) by working on a board before you attempt to paint the flowerpot. Time spent experimenting with technique and colour is time well spent. When you are confident with the technique, start spattering your pot.

4 When the spattered paint is completely dry, varnish it with two coats of matt or satin finish exterior-grade varnish.

the basic technique

Dip the tip of your paintbrush lightly in
the paint. Holding the brush in your
right hand and a heavy stick in your
left, strike the loaded brush against the
stick, aiming the paint at the pot. Wear
overalls, eye protection and cover your
hair because, until you learn control of
the technique, paint will fly in all
directions. This is why it is advisable to
use water-soluble emulsion paints only.

From now on it's up to you. Enjoy
yourself, using as many colours as you
can lay your hands on. Spattering is an
inexact art but the general rules are:
• The more paint you load on your
brush, the larger the spots of colour
you will create
• The drier the brush the smaller the
spots created
• Very wet paint will result in messy
indistinct spots, which will have a
tendency to run
• Take it slowly and allow colours to
build up and dry before adding too
many further colours
• Keep turning the pot and spatter
paint from different heights and angles
• Try not to create too many lines of
any one colour on the pot
• Try not to touch the pot until it is
completely dry. Large spots take longer
to dry
• Try using contrasting colours and
sizes of spatter. (Larger spots of bright
red can look very effective with a
muted basic colour range.)
• If you make a mistake it doesn't
matter. Carry on overlaying colours until
the end result you want is achieved, or
repaint with charcoal grey paint and
start again.

1

2

antique gold pots

Small flowerpots can be attractively decorated with gold leaf, but the process is quite complex and the materials are expensive. We illustrate here how a similar effect can be achieved using gold paint or paste. Gold paint or paste is available in many tones – you could also experiment with different coloured metal paints including bronze and silver.

Grouped together in an old seed tray with a night light or candle in each, these pots make an eye-catching table display, perfect for alfresco dining.

materials
Terracotta flowerpot
Red oxide primer
Gold paint or paste
Fine-grade emery paper or wire wool
Dark shellac varnish or exterior-grade
  medium wood stain varnish

equipment
25mm (1in) paintbrush

1 Place your hand inside the flowerpot and carefully paint the outside with red oxide primer. When completely dry, apply a good-quality gold paint or paste.

2 Allow the metallic paint or paste to dry thoroughly (for at least 24 hours). Rub areas on the pot, such as the rims, where natural wear would occur, using fine emery paper or wire wool to reveal the red oxide and terracotta beneath the gold paint. Finish the pot by applying a coat of dark shellac varnish or a stained varnish.

white-washed pots

Old clay flowerpots often display an attractive patina of white efflorescence on their exterior. Here is a simple method for emulating this natural finish on new terracotta pots.

materials
New terracotta flowerpot
White matt emulsion paint
White spirit

equipment
Disposable rubber gloves (optional)
25mm (1in) paintbrush
Clean cotton rags

1 It is a good idea to wear disposable rubber gloves for this project. Select a new terracotta pot, ideally one with a raised rim or pattern, and paint the exterior liberally with white matt emulsion paint. Make sure it is fully covered with paint and take care to cover all the recesses.

2 Rub off the wet white paint immediately with a clean cotton rag, leaving a residue of paint in any indentations in the pot. Hold the pot under running water for a minute or so and then, with a new piece of clean rag, wipe off most of the remaining paint from the surface of the pot.

3 The appearance you seek to accomplish is a soft dusty white that covers the pot's surface with irregular areas of more solid colour in the recesses and indentations. If you are not satisfied with the result you have achieved, wash the pot again before the paint is fully dry and repeat the process.

4 This technique works particularly well with aqua green paint to simulate a washed verdigris finish.

textured pots

Modern terracotta or plastic pots can be embellished in a number of eye-catching ways by applying a variety of decorations. You can use plaster mouldings, wooden or plastic shapes (available from good hobby, craft or decorator's shops), shells, pebbles, driftwood or even nuts and bolts or old keys for a highly individual look. Here we have used shells picked up on our local beach for one pot, and two thicknesses of rope for a uniquely textured appearance on the other pot.

Both pots have been painted stark white but you may prefer to use a two-tone finish to highlight the textures of the decoration.

materials

Plastic or terracotta flowerpots
Builder's adhesive or waterproof
   tile cement
Variety of sea shells or two thicknesses
   of rope
White matt emulsion paint
Exterior-grade matt varnish

equipment

25mm (1in) stiff paintbrush

1 To decorate the pot using rope, first measure the circumference at the top and cut a piece of thick rope to this length. Decide on the position of the thin rope, measure and cut four lengths of rope to fit around the pot. Apply builder's adhesive or tile cement directly on to the back of the thick rope and place it in position just below the rim of the pot. Attach the thin rope in the same way. Allow the adhesive to dry before painting. Apply two coats of white matt emulsion paint. When this is dry, seal the pot with two coats of exterior-grade matt varnish. Use a stiff brush to apply both the paint and varnish, making sure that all nooks and crannies are well covered.

2 For the shell-decorated pot, place a liberal amount of builder's adhesive or tile cement on to the back of each shell and attach the shell to the pot. If you are using tile cement, you can paste a small area at a time, attach some shells and then add more cement and decoration as you work around the surface of the pot. Leave to dry thoroughly. Paint as in step 1.

inspirational ideas

Indulge your whims and create your own garden ornaments. Install a garden clock on an

outhouse wall, wield secateurs to clip fantastic topiary shapes in hedges or potted shrubs, build

a fountain or ransack a local reclamation yard for objects that you can utilize in your garden.

Be innovative and never frightened to experiment with unusual uses for everyday items.

Incorporate old drainpipes in planting schemes, use reclaimed tiles to construct tall planters or

use tiles and slates to edge a flowerbed. If not too costly, salvage gates and iron fencing for repair

and rejuvenation and always keep your eyes open for a cast-off or undervalued object that could

become a focal point in your garden.

Remember that you have vertical as well as horizontal surfaces in your garden. Walls can support a trellis framework bought from a garden centre or one made yourself to the required size and shape from old wooden pallets stripped of nails and staples and stained, painted or treated with a wood preservative wash. A trellis screen can be the perfect solution for hiding an unsightly area of waste bins or compost heaps. Alternatively, for a less obtrusive look, stretch dark green gardener's wire on nails driven into fences and walls, over which climbers such as honeysuckle, clematis and roses will grow and clamber.

Aside from plants, why not hang a decorative wall plaque or a pagan mask to add an element of interest or surprise, or incorporate an old arabesque door or carved window in an otherwise plain wall? Attractive wall decorations made from stone, lead, resin and frost-proof terracotta can be found in garden and craft centres and are also available from individual makers who are often only too happy to make a commissioned design. Why not consider, too, commissioning a sculpture, possibly a life-size creation in chicken wire of your favourite animal or indulge an obsession for creating your own outdoor sculpture gallery?

above *Home-made and stained trellis bedecked with evergreen honeysuckle and rambling kiwi fruit hides unsightly plastic-covered compost bins*

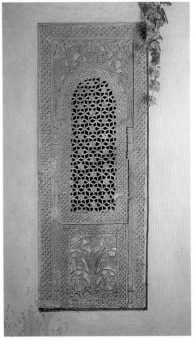

above *A Goan carved alabaster window inserted in the gable end wall of a newly constructed summerhouse*

above A sculpted stone "mother and child" placed casually on a plinth of natural stone is half-hidden by foliage inside a walled garden

right A carved slate fountain surmounted by cast bronze birds

Arches in wood or metal, woven willow wigwams, pergolas and obelisks can be architectural ornaments or features in themselves, unadorned by greenery. Small gardens can be dark but, with careful planting in warm bright tones, one can give the illusion of sunshine to dark areas, backed by the clever use of a mirror to give the feeling of a much larger space. Alternatively, a wall painted in a bold colour will create a sunny outlook, especially during the winter months.

Define borders in your garden with scallop shells, rope or old tiles salvaged from a reclamation yard; use a metal finial discovered in a junk shop to add the final touch to a greenhouse or display old garden tools on a whitewashed wall. Whatever you do, be original and impose your own personality on your outdoor space. Create surprises, use unusual objects in unpredictable places.

left *A seating area in a small urban garden has been made to seem much larger by the clever use of a small bamboo-framed mirror*

above *Reclamation yards yield a whole host of items such as the iron gates and . fencing in the top picture. The stacked old terracotta ridge tiles show all the colours of lichen growth and ageing*

right *Cast-iron gutter hoppers fixed to an iron wheel and planted with geraniums make an imaginative wall display*

flowerpot topiary

Ivies grown in a flowerpot and trained into topiary forms make wonderful table decorations and you might well find that this project leads to an absorbing hobby. Trimmed with bows and ribbons, or even embellished with tiny coloured lights, such topiary will enhance any outdoor festive table.

The metal form used here was bought from a florist, but any shape can be used and it is simple to construct your own frame from mesh or wire and a metal rod or bar, moulded and tied with twists of garden wire. Pick a plant with several long tendrils and when it is trained, pinch off the growing ends to stimulate thicker growth and remove any larger leaves to encourage small-leaf development. Experiment with different shapes: balls and cones are simple, animal and bird shapes more challenging, while hoops and spirals are easy to construct and rewarding in their end result.

We have used a plastic pot for this project. If you use a terracotta pot, the existing drainage hole will be adequate as is.

materials
250mm (10in) terracotta or plastic
  flowerpot
0.5kg (1lb) sharp gravel or small stones
1kg (2lb) sand and cement mix
100mm (4in) length of 15mm (⅝in)
  copper tubing
Florist's decorative metal shape
600mm (2ft) length of 10 x 2mm
  (⅜ x ¹⁄₁₆in) iron bar
Medium gardener's wire

equipment
Electric drill, for plastic pot
8mm (⅝in) drill bit, for plastic pot
Pliers

planting
Potting compost
1 or 2 trailing ivies, or similar plants
Fine gardener's wire

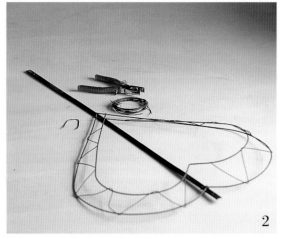

1   If you are using a plastic flowerpot with no drainage hole, drill an 8mm (⅝in) diameter hole in the middle of the base of the pot. Add the gravel to the sand and cement and mix with enough water to give a wet consistency. Place the copper piping in the base of the pot over the drainage hole. Pour in the wet sand and cement mix to just under the top of the copper pipe. Ensure the pipe is vertical and leave the cement to set.

2   Fix the florist's shape securely to the iron bar using medium gardener's wire and pliers. When the cement is fully dry, stand the iron bar in the copper pipe.

3   Fill the pot with potting compost and plant the ivy, packing the compost firmly around its roots. Twist the longest tendrils of the ivy up and around the metal bar to the base of the decorative florist's shape, and weave tendrils in, out and around the shape to emphasize the form. Once the shape is covered to your satisfaction, pinch off any loose growing ends of ivy to promote thicker growth. Loose tendrils can be secured to the shape with fine gardener's wire. Any short tendrils of ivy can be allowed to flow over the sides of the pot.

4   Water and feed your flowerpot topiary regularly. You will find that misting with water from a hand spray will be beneficial, too.

materials

Strong *Lonicera nitida* plant with
    long shoots
Potting mixture of soil and compost
    or well-rotted farmyard manure
Grit, for drainage
Water-retaining granules
Long-lasting fertilizer granules
Liquid fertilizer

equipment

Garden shears
250mm (10in) flowerpot

evergreen topiary bird

Topiary, the art of clipping hedging into ornamental shapes, predates the Romans. Its popularity has ebbed and flowed with changes in garden fashion but reached its peak in Victorian times when many English country houses sported topiary gardens and wondrous beasts adorned many cottage hedges.

As interior design is extended into our gardens, topiary is once again fashionable and, armed with shears and a little patience, the creative gardener can have a lot of fun persuading bushes into geometric shapes such as balls or cones that, with regular cutting, can become surprisingly satisfactory features. If, however, you aspire to something a little more whimsical such as a plump hen or a strutting peacock, the best shrubs to work with are box, yew or the fast-growing honeysuckle, *Lonicera nitida*.

The first two are fairly stiff plants, which can in time be transformed into magnificent robust shapes and can be hurried along with weekly liquid feeding and a lot of watering during the growing season. *Lonicera nitida* grows quite happily in a pot, is pliable, easy to work and will produce a fairly complex shape within a relatively short time.

Strong healthy *Lonicera nitida* plants are available from nurseries and garden centres and can be found in two varieties – gold or dark green. Select one with long angular shoots and follow the instructions below to create a topiary bird.

1 Pot your *Lonicera nitida* in a mixture of soil and compost. Place your potted plant on a flat surface at about waist height. Stand back and carefully observe its shape. This is probably the most important part of the project because it will determine the eventual shape of your topiary bird. Look for any strong shoots that will form a possible neck or tail. A curvaceous shoot might be the beginning of a cockerel's tail, an upright one might be transformed into a goose's neck. If nothing suggests itself, gently part the foliage and look again.

2 Once you have decided on a general shape, gather the shoots to be made into the neck of the bird and gently plait them together. Repeat to make a tail, if there is to be one. Stand back and look at the plant again. If something else now suggests itself, start again. When you have decided on the final shape of your bird, plait the shoots gently but firmly; finish braiding to the tip of the shoot and then bend into the desired shape.

3 Tuck in any loose shoots and clip back straggly growth to the main frame. Look again at your creation and make sure that it is secure and well trimmed to its intended shape. Good topiary must have a firm foundation.

4 Now you must ensure the plant will grow, so feed and water it well. As it grows, repot it into a larger container, using a potting mixture of soil, compost or well-rotted farmyard manure, a little grit for drainage, some water-retaining granules and some long-lasting fertilizer granules. Spray the plant weekly with liquid fertilizer during the growing season. Cut it back regularly to its original shape after 25mm (1in) growth has occurred, to retain its original size. To allow it to grow larger, cut back 25mm (1in) after 50mm (2in) has grown, as this will maintain a strong body. If you make a mistake, don't despair – your plant will soon regrow its shape.

5 If you wish to enlarge your plant even further, continue replanting it in larger pots and periodically replace the surface of the soil, adding more long-lasting fertilizer. Maintain leaf growth with liquid fertilizer and keep the new growth trimmed to shape.

wire heart

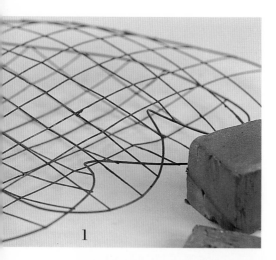

Sculptured floral displays can be some of the most striking and attractive of garden ornamentation. Whether planted with growing flowering and foliage plants, each in a plug of growing compound inserted in sphagnum moss, or with cut flowers or leaves embedded in florist's medium to make a dazzling temporary display, wire shapes can be transformed into almost any number of unusual hanging decorations, perfect for suspending above a table set for a candlelit outdoor dinner, or from a balcony or outdoor pergola.

For this project we used wire heart shapes purchased from a florist, which can be used time and time again, and used leaves and flowers to make a temporary floral display. These welded wire shapes are charming in their own right and are now fast being superseded by less expensive moulded shapes. Most florists still hold stocks of these old shapes and are willing to sell them at very reasonable prices, but if you are unsuccessful in securing them, similar shapes can be constructed from wire netting, moulded into shape and fastened with florist's wire.

materials

Two welded wire florist's heart shapes
Florist's wire
Oasis or other florist's display medium
Length of 12mm (½in) plated metal
    link chain
Two 25mm (1in) spring (lanyard) hooks
Metal "S" hook
Cut foliage or flowers

equipment

Pliers or wire cutters
Long-bladed serrated knife

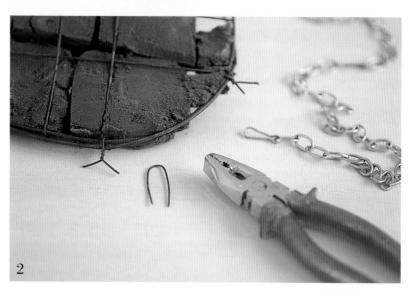

1 Carefully bend the centres of the wire shapes to make two matching concave hearts. With the insides facing, secure the hearts together with wire ties on one side only, allowing the shapes to be separated so as to allow the florist's medium to be inserted.

2 Cut your florist's display medium into shapes to fit inside your heart. Try to keep the pieces as large as possible. Continue to fill the wire-framed heart until the entire shape is filled. Gently close the halves together over the medium and secure them together with more florist's wire. Use a serrated knife to trim off any protruding medium, forced out of the shapes when the halves are closed together.

3 Place the completed heart in cold water until the medium is fully saturated. Secure the two ends of your chain to the heart using the 25mm (1in) spring hooks. Hang the heart above a sink or bowl from the "S" hook, until the excess water has drained away. Gently insert your cut foliage or flowers into the medium until the whole shape is covered. Make sure that as far as possible the cut ends of the plants do not protrude through the medium.

maintenance

You will need to water your floral
display daily as the water will slowly
drain from your shape, be evaporated
by the atmosphere and absorbed by the
plants. Position your display where it
can hang and drain freely and add the
water from the top. A floral feed can be
added to the water for extra benefit.

recycled wall planters

Any number of reclaimed materials can be used in your garden: old tyres stacked to make a container for potatoes or invasive mint, which would otherwise overrun the surrounding area, wooden pallets transformed into compost containers or timber salvaged to make fencing, trellis or garden furniture. We have even seen an old bicycle wheel mounted on a pole and secured to the ground with wire on which grew a profusion of highly scented sweet peas.

Many items salvaged from a builder's reclamation yard can be transformed into striking and useful containers for a collection of growing plants. Iron drain hoppers make useful wall planters, chimney pots convert into excellent tall pots and even old windows can be put to good use to make forcing beds for young seedlings.

For this project we used a selection of old terracotta hip tiles to make into wall planters. Hip tiles are usually triangular in shape and are designed to secure the joins in a roof against the worst of the wind and weather. They are the ideal shape for wall planters and come in as many sizes and patterns as there are varieties of roof tiles. Less than 100 years ago, in areas where clay could be found, almost every small town and village boasted a brick and tile works where often quite whimsical tiles, finials and even garden ornaments were manufactured. The catalogues published by these old companies advertise a bewildering selection of both practical and fanciful terracotta.

materials
Old terracotta roof hip tile
Fine-guage chicken wire
Three 50mm (2in) long 6mm (¼in) zinc
    plated or other weather-resistant
    screws and 3 medium rawlplugs, for
    hanging the planter

equipment
Electric drill
6mm (¼in) masonry drill bit
Waste timber or board
Pencil

1 Examine your old terracotta tile for any existing nail fixing holes. Most hip tiles are fixed with nails although some more modern types may have lugs or protrusions moulded on to the rear, which are designed to fit into a rebate on the next tile above to hold it in place. It is advisable to secure hip tile wall planters with fixing holes at three points – at the apex of the triangular shape and at the two outer edges where the tile will sit against the vertical surface on which it will be mounted. Lay your tile, concave side up, on a piece of waste timber or board and mark the points where you wish to drill the holes. Hold the drill vertically and carefully drill at slow speed through to the scrap material underneath. Terracotta is a relatively fragile material so it needs treating with care: hold the tile tightly down on to your waste surface, do not use the drill's hammer action and be careful to drill slowly so as to minimize the chances of the tile cracking or the terracotta breaking away where the drill bit emerges.

2 Choose the site for your wall planter with care, remembering that when hung and planted it will need regular watering, and soil and water will inevitably leak from the bottom of the tile. Place the planter in position and mark the holes required on the wall's surface. If a stone, brick or solid wall surface is used, it will be necessary to drill and insert medium rawlplugs in the wall before fixing the planter *in situ* with screws. Use zinc-plated or other corrosion-resistant screws and do not over-tighten them or you may crack the terracotta.

3 When the planter is in position, fold and bend a piece of fine-gauge chicken wire into a shape to fit the bottom of the tile. Place it inside the planter to help prevent soil being washed out of the planter when it is watered. The planter is now ready for use. Fill it with soil or potting compost to approximately 12mm (½in) below the rim of the tile and add a suitable colourful or trailing plant, like the wild strawberries shown here.

garden markers

Old seed packets stuck on top of a stick, faded with the sun and battered by wind and rain can look unsightly. None the less, it is useful to know which variety of flower or vegetable is planted where, on what date the crop will require thinning, or when the next application of fertilizer is due. Functional garden markers are essential to the organized gardener and, if imaginatively made, will add interest and appeal to any garden scheme. Attractive as well as practical, these will fast become a garden essential.

The markers shown here are simply made from offcut timber but could just as easily be made from any number of other materials. Keep a good stock of markers, both tall ones for your herbaceous borders and vegetable garden and shorter ones for practical use in the greenhouse, potting shed or vegetable garden.

Let your imagination run riot and try different shapes and colours when making garden markers. Children particularly will enjoy displaying markers in their own private garden plots. Encourage them to design and make their own, and help nurture the next generation of gardeners. Uncomplicated shapes are always best – try cats, dogs and other simply drawn animal shapes. Stars and moons are ever popular and if you have a particular artistic bent, why not make markers in the shape of the vegetable or flower growing where the marker is placed?

materials

Offcut timber – approx. 12mm (½in) thick for the shapes and 18 x 18mm (¾ x ¾in) for the stakes
Waterproof PVA glue
25mm (1in) panel pins
Medium and fine-grade glasspaper
Selection of coloured preservative water-based wood stains and matt emulsion or artist's acrylic tube paints
Blackboard paint or black matt emulsion paint

equipment

Band saw, jig saw or fret saw
Hammer
25mm (1in) paintbrush

1 Using a band, jig or fret saw cut out rectangles, squares, stars (or any other shapes), out of the 12mm (½in) thick offcut timber. Glue and nail these shapes to various lengths of sharpened stakes cut from approximately 18 x 18mm (¾ x ¾in) offcut timber.

2 Paint the assembled markers with coloured preservative wood stains. Experiment with colours, mixing stains or making your own colours using watered down emulsion or artist's acrylic tube paints mixed with water-based wood preservative. When the stain is dry, sand the front of the markers to a smooth surface and paint with blackboard paint or black matt emulsion paint.

3 Hold your marker by its stake and press firmly into the ground in its chosen location. Write on it using moistened chalk to identify a species, or give a planting or harvesting date or other information.

materials

Old wooden glazed window frame

Paint stripper

Length of 100 x 18mm (4 x ¾in) planed
    softwood timber, to fit inside frame

Two pieces of 6mm (¼in) plywood or
    chip (particle) board sheet, to fit frame

Length of 50 x 25mm (2 x 1in) rough-
    sawn timber, to fit frame (battens)

Waterproof PVA glue

40mm (1½in) cross-head screws

Wood filler

Buff-coloured matt emulsion paint

Crackle glaze

Self-adhesive plastic Roman numerals

Antique pine liquid wax

Four waterproof (outdoor-quality)
    electric clock mechanisms, hands
    and batteries

18mm (¾in) zinc-plated cross-head
    screws

Length of self-adhesive window
    draft-proofing strip, to fit frame

Two brass mirror plates, for hanging
    the clock

18mm (¾in) brass screws

Black and white matt emulsion paint

Antique pine furniture wax

Exterior-grade varnish

equipment

Try square

Metal scraper

Medium-grade glasspaper

Tape measure

Pencil

Hand saw

Cross-head screwdriver

Awl or sharp point

Electric drill

10mm (⅜in) spade bit

3mm (⅛in) drill bit

25mm (1in) paintbrush

50mm (2in) soft paintbrush

Clean cotton rags

Straight edge

window pane clock

Like many people today we have a widely spread family and numerous friends who live abroad. Britain has Greenwich Mean Time (GMT), Summer Time and has experimented with Daylight Saving Time, while Continental European time is one hour later, except at certain times of year when it is the same. America has five time zones, Canada six and Australia three. Doing business abroad can be baffling enough and in today's shrinking world different time zones can create confusion and frustration.

We thought of keeping several clocks to help when dealing with the local times of family, friends and customers abroad. The desire to keep a record of several different time zones became the justification for this window pane clock, a rationale for turning what was initially a fun idea into a practical reality.

If you do not have an old window frame you could make a wooden frame with as many "panes" (time zones) as you wish. Battery-driven clock mechanisms are readily available and very inexpensive. Make sure, however, that you use waterproof mechanisms, that the clock is sealed thoroughly to protect it from the wind and the rain and that you situate your clock in a relatively sheltered position.

3

4

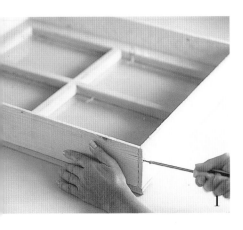
1

2

1 Strip the old window frame of paint and make sure the timber is sound and the putty and glass intact. Remove any hinges or nails. Cut four lengths of 100 x 18mm (4 x ¾in) planed softwood timber to make a frame to fit inside the rebate behind the window, ensuring its outer edge is flush with the outside of the window frame. Fix with glue and 40mm (1½in) screws, the heads driven below the surface of the timber. Fill the screw head holes with wood filler and sand to a smooth finish.

2 Cut two pieces of 6mm (¼in) plywood or chip (particle) board to fit flush inside the frame. On one piece mark with pencil the position of the window panes, marking the corners of each with a sharp point or awl so they will be visible when the board is painted. Mark the centre of each pane and cut a 10mm (⅜in) hole through the board at these points with a spade drill bit. Paint the board with one coat of buff matt emulsion paint and allow to dry. Paint over the emulsion paint with

crackle glaze and allow to dry thoroughly. Mix two parts of white matt emulsion paint with one part water. With steady even strokes, carefully paint over the glazed board, using a 50mm (2in) soft paintbrush. Try not to over-paint previous brush strokes or the glaze will pull and leave an unsightly finish. As the second coat of paint dries, cracks will begin to appear, allowing the colour of the first coat to show through. When the paint is fully dry, join the previously marked corners using a pencil and a straight edge to make four clock faces. Mark each clock dial and apply the self-adhesive plastic Roman numerals.

3 Paint over the board with antique pine liquid wax, immediately dabbing at it with a clean cotton cloth to remove the excess. Do not wipe off the wax too vigorously or the crackle finish will be damaged. Insert the clock mechanisms through the drilled holes from the rear and attach the hands and batteries, setting the clocks for the desired times. Place the board, clock faces down, into the bottom of the

boxed frame. Cut four lengths of 50 x 25m (2 x 1in) rough-sawn timber to make battens to fit inside the frame so as to hold the clock board down. Fix the battens using 40mm (1½in) screws driven into the sides of the frame .

4 Place the second 6mm (¼in) board in the the frame, resting it on the fixed battens. Fix the board to the battens with 18mm (¾in) zinc-plated cross-head screws then attach a self-adhesive window draft-proofing strip on top to give the unit a damp-resistant seal all round. Using 18mm (¾in) brass screws, fit the brass mirror plates securely to the top of the timber frame, roughly 50mm (2in) from each side.

5 Paint the clock with black matt emulsion paint. When dry, sand the edges to simulate age and wear and apply antique pine furniture wax vigorously with a cotton rag. Leave to dry then buff to a shine with more cotton rags. This finish is fairly weather-resistant, but for a fully weatherproof finish, give the clock at least three coats of exterior-grade varnish instead.

slate fountain

1 Dig a trench for the electrical power supply leading to the site. (Use an outdoor socket or waterproof junction box for the power supply.) Dig a 150mm (6in) deep hole with gently sloping sides, the base to be about 1.3m x 900mm (4ft 4in x 3ft). Within the hole and about 150mm (6in) from one corner, dig a second hole the size of your reservoir tank. Adjacent to this hole, dig a 150mm (6in) deep hole, approximately 400mm (1ft 4in) square. Insert the plastic reservoir tank in the second hole, leaving about 25mm (1in) above the surface. Fill the third hole with concrete mix to make a base for the slate fountain structure. Level the surface and leave the concrete to set.

2 Line the sides and base of the 1.3m x 900mm (4ft 4in x 3ft) hole to a depth of 25mm (1in) with sand, and cover with a polythene pond liner. Cut a hole in the liner over the top of the reservoir ensuring that the liner overlaps the reservoir tank sides by at least 50mm (2in). To form the concrete base for the fountain, construct a simple 300 x 300 x 150mm (12 x 12 x 6in) square or angled box from shuttering or plywood. Drill a hole in the centre of one side using a 20mm (⅞in) spade bit. Using a hand saw, cut out a 20mm (⅞in) wide "U" section below the drilled hole to allow the shuttering to be removed over the pipe once the concrete within it has set. Place the box on top of the existing concrete base with the "U" section facing down and towards the reservoir. Join the two lengths of metal piping with an "L" bend elbow joint and place the whole piece in the box with the

shorter length passing through the "U" section and over the reservoir. Fill the box to its surface with more concrete mix making sure the longer metal pipe remains vertical in the concrete. Leave it to set.

3 Remove the wooden casing from the set concrete. Place the water pump in the reservoir and connect the plastic pipe to the metal pipe. Connect the pump to the electrical supply and place the metal grill over the top of the reservoir. Using the 20mm (⅞in) masonry bit, drill holes to take the copper piping in the centre of the slate

Water can be one of the most important features of garden ornamentation and running water adds the fascination of movement and sound to what will undoubtedly be the focal point of any design.

Whether purely decorative or as a home for fish and water plants, ponds offer refuge for a wide variety of garden wildlife as well as being a constant source of enjoyment for the garden lover. There are an enormous range of commercially made plastic pond liners, water pumps and other materials available from good garden stores, yet striking water features can be constructed from the most simple and readily available materials. An old bath sunk into the ground and surrounded by paving to break its shape makes a practical pond; a wooden barrel, cut in half and filled with water and flowering lilies will enhance any patio and a waterfall fed by an electrically powered recirculating pump and constructed from stone slabs will add charm to any garden.

Landscape designer, Ben Pike, designed this slate fountain to be simple to construct and easy to maintain. His essentially contemporary design can be adapted to suit a number of different materials or locations..

slabs. Build the fountain by sliding each slate slab over the vertical metal pipe on to the concrete base and securing with a generous application of waterproof mastic.

4 Fill the large lined hole with loose cobbles to just above the surrounding surface level and fill the reservoir with water. Turn on the pump and enjoy your creation.

maintenance

Evaporation and natural wastage will soon diminish the water supply in the reservoir. It is simple to construct a dip stick, which can be inserted into the reservoir through the cobbles to check the water level. Check the level and top up periodically. The reservoir may be filled by pouring water through the cobbles, there is no need to remove cobbles to reveal the reservoir other than for six-monthly periodic cleaning.

IMPORTANT SAFETY NOTE – This project requires an outdoor electrical feed for the water pump. Water and electricity can be an extremely dangerous mixture! It is important that every care is taken in supplying electrical feed to the pump and professional help should be sought to check the safety of the wiring.

materials

Plastic water reservoir tank, approx.
  600mm² (2ft sq) and
  400mm (1ft 4in) deep
Concrete mix
Sand
Polythene pond liner
Four 300mm (12in) lengths of 150 x
  18mm (6 x ¾in) shuttering board or
  plywood
40mm (1½in) cut or oval nails
815mm (2ft 8in) length of 18mm (¾in)
  copper or galvanized steel piping, cut
  into:
  200mm (8in) length
  600mm (2ft) length
18mm (¾in) copper or galvanized steel
  "L" bend elbow joint
18mm (¾in) metal-to-plastic pipe
  connector
18mm (¾in) plastic water pipe
Submersible water pump
  (60 watt is ideal)
25mm (1in) galvanized metal grill
Quantity of slate
Waterproof mastic
Quantity of cobbles

equipment

Spade
Shovel, for mixing concrete
Craft knife
Hammer
Electric drill
20mm (⅞in) spade bit
20mm (⅞in) masonry bit
Hand saw
Hacksaw
Mastic gun

sources and techniques

The owner of your local reclamation or salvage yard will be a fund of expert information. He will have in stock, or know where to find, almost anything you may need to make any number of original garden constructions or ornaments.

Many of the projects in this book require timber and the use of stains, paints, finishes and varnishes. Most of these items can be purchased from local timber or builder's merchants or do-it-yourself stores, but here we share a few simple techniques. A little research will reveal various other sources of materials and techniques that might not be immediately apparent.

Rough-sawn timber can be bought as offcut material from many timber merchants. Large commercial customers require timber cut to exact sizes and the waste resulting from this sizing can be purchased very inexpensively, often for just the cost of removing it. Sawmills are another useful source of timber. Logged softwood is put through the mill and the outer trimmings, often with bark still attached, if not sold, are pulped, chipped or used as firewood.

using colour

Colour plays an important part in our lives: in fashion, interiors and gardens among others. In nature colour is everywhere. The strong striking shades of a hot summer's day sky can range from cobalt blue through to the sunset shades of vermilion and bright orange. Another day the sky may be overcast and grey paling to silver, or charcoal with a storm threatening. Foliage is made up of hundreds of different shades of green, from emerald and olive green to khaki; and the colours of flowers and fruits are vibrant jewel-like shades of purple, scarlet, burgundy, rich dark cherry red or vivid yellow. The earth ranges in colour from the blue-greys of clay through the chocolate-browns of loam and the black of peat to the tan and cinnamon hues of sand. So look again at the beauty of the landscape around us that we all take so much for granted.

In northern countries we have been nervous in the past of using bold colours in our gardens, remaining conservative in our tastes and unwilling to experiment. This is slowly changing as a result of increased travel opportunities, and exposure to other cultures has become a strong influence. The information on gardens and interiors and the way they inter-relate, which now comes in abundance from books, newspapers, magazines and television, has, if anything, influenced us too far the other way, persuading us to use too much colour at times, to no great effect. Whether we choose a random colour scheme or opt for a coordinated look in our gardens, there are endless ways of using colour.

Colour can vary greatly in different lights and spaces. There is no reason why you should not change the colour of your garden accessories to blend in with the

above *A display of grasses in muted colours, growing in old and weathered terracotta containers*

right *A group of cacti planted in gravel and pebbles offset by one stone, painted red and strategically placed. An old Dutch stoneware gin bottle stands in the background*

seasons. In spring you might dress your garden table in yellows and greens with floral or striped tablecloths, crockery in primrose or daffodil yellow, tumblers in grasshopper green and the first of the narcissi or hyacinths as a table centrepiece.

In high summer, when the sky is at its most blue, tubs, troughs and containers can be painted in strong Mediterranean blues or greens. You could use both colours, one painted on top of the other with the underneath colour showing through. This is a good combination, particularly if planted with flowers in hot colours of pink and orange. Garden chairs and benches and even the old potting shed can be given a new lease of life with a vibrant coat of colour or, if your preference is for more subtle muted shades, try blue-greys and grey-greens instead, which look very pretty with terracottas and russets.

Autumn and falling leaves suggest tints of rust, gold, beige and bronze and call for classic Madras plaid for tablecloths and napkins. Use coordinating cushions and throws in colours of cinnamon, ginger, coral and yellow ochre. Bare branches, twigs and cinnamon sticks look stunning displayed in earthenware pots for a late summer outdoor lunch, offset by collections of pebbles, driftwood, shells and pine cones that catch the soft autumnal light and add texture to a display. Do not forget, either, that, giant flame-coloured pumpkins with cut-out faces illuminated by candles can be placed around the garden in time for Halloween.

Finally, there is winter, when large, inexpensive plastic pots can be painted white and filled with evergreens, topiary or silver-grey shrubs for a brave statement. Stylish zinc or aluminum containers are probably more practical, but then again, why not feel free to do whatever takes the mood?

above *A modest garden shed has been given a new lease of life with a large picture window and clever use of an attractive colour wash paint finish*

paints and stains

A basic knowledge of different paints and stains is essential for anyone wishing to make or transform garden ornaments, or indeed pursue any other form of painting and decorating. There follows an outline of the varieties of paints and stains commercially available and their uses.

paints

Commercially available paints are generally either water based or spirit based. Various other paints can be made from milk or linseed oil, using earth or other pigments, and a mention should be made of limewashes and distempers, which are still available from specialist paint and decorator's shops and are well worth experimenting with for their soft, subtle chalky effect. They are particularly suited for use on substrates that need to breathe.

Water-based paints are easy to use. Modern paint technology has produced water-based gloss paints, which have obvious advantages, and their manufacturers claim that their strength, longevity and resistance to fade are equal to that of oil-based paints. Another commonly used water-based paint is acrylic combined primer undercoat – again very useful and quick drying although we do prefer separate oil-based wood primers and undercoats when gloss painting.

The most useful water-based paints are the modern acrylic emulsion paints, available in literally thousand of colours, including numerous authentic period shades. In matt or silk (semi-gloss) finish, either off the shelf or mixed to match, these paints are a boon to the modern decorator. Although not recommended by their manufacturers for outside use, if properly protected with an exterior-grade varnish, emulsion paints can be used for most outside purposes.

Modern oil-based paints are generally obtainable in gloss or satin (semi-gloss) finishes, although a limited selection of matt (or flat) finishes can also be purchased. White spirit, turpentine or turpentine substitute are necessary for brush cleaning, as well as for any spillage or drips. For convenience, many of these paints are now sold in a "non-drip" form. The colours available are almost as many as for emulsion paints and, although slower drying than water-based paints, the semi-gloss paints can dry surprisingly quickly. Oil-based paints should generally be applied over an appropriate undercoat.

Experiment with mixing paints. Add colour from tubes of artist's paints, acrylic for water-based paints and oil tube paint for spirit-based paints, or even liquid stains to achieve your own shades. Remember, however, that you may not be able to recreate that exact shade again and certain colours, particularly blues and reds, are "fugitive" and may fade with time.

A variety of specialist paints will prove useful for finishing garden furniture, ornaments and accessories. Some are formulated for use with particular metals, others for glass or ceramics. Red oxide, the prescribed paint for rust-proofing iron and steel has recently been superseded by a number of extremely effective proprietary iron primers, some requiring their own solvent. Look over the shelves of your local do-it-yourself store or paint retailer, read the labels on the paints and never be afraid of asking advice.

far left *Strings of onions hung on a limewashed greenhouse wall*

centre left *White gloss paint offset by black metalwork looks exceptionally attractive on this simple wooden arch-top gate*

left *The faded door of an old cider barn shows little evidence of its original bright blue paintwork. The small cut-out door is proof of its one-time use as a henhouse*

stains

Stains can be divided into three categories: fence stains or paints, transparent stains and opaque stains. Whichever type of stain you use, be sure it has been formulated specifically for use on exterior timber. Many exterior stains will contain timber preservative, but excellent stains can be made from using transparent timber preservative and concentrated liquid or powder "non-fugitive" wood stains.

Fence stains come in a limited number of colours. Largely designed to emulate the so-called "natural" colours of timber, together with a few other popular shades, they are usually water based and easy to use. Always read and follow the manufacturer's recommendations for use and application.

Transparent stains are either water or spirit based. Water-based stains are most useful for use on rough-sawn or planed timber, but have a tendency to raise the grain on planed timber. To achieve maximum penetration and an even finish, water-based stains must be applied to dry timber. Spirit-based stains tend to penetrate wood better, give a more solid colour and dry extremely quickly. Care should be taken, however, to apply the stain evenly or an uneven finish will result. A specialist wood paint shop will reveal a bewildering selection of concentrated water- and spirit-based wood stains and dyes from which to select your colours.

A recent development in stains has been the introduction of new opaque water- and spirit-based wood stains. Sold in a selection of colours, these stains can be mixed to almost any imaginable shade and are very easy to use. Particularly useful for planed timber, they are made in interior and outdoor formulations and offer excellent cover and colour saturation. We have used these stains on various projects in this book with excellent results.

Concentrated transparent and opaque liquid stains can be used to paint canvas or other materials and are ideally suited for decorating canvas or deckchairs, or adding colour and pattern to the hammock on page 22.

left *An attractively stained wooden fence makes the perfect backdrop for this ingeniously displayed selection of plants in modern terracotta pots*

simple finishes

Paint finishing is a whole subject in itself. Should you wish for a more "in-depth" knowledge of paint techniques and to pursue this fascinating topic further, there are any number of informative books on decorating everything from pots and containers to wall surfaces, garden furniture and even plastic statuary, to disguise its origins. Here we can only whet your appetite with a few simple, tried and tested techniques.

"ocean drift" finish

This finish is designed to be used on old or rough-sawn timber in order to show off the natural grain of the wood, emphasize its character and simulate the bleaching effects of wind and weather softened by time. It is an infinitely variable finish, which with experimentation can produce a number of different effects, ranging from nearly white to a dark, almost scorched wood effect. Try different approaches to preparing the original wood substrate, for example varying finishes can be achieved by staining the bare wood before painting. A smoother wood surface will give a less dramatic colour contrast; using less paint and waxing while the paint is wet will give a soft finish that accentuates the wood's natural colour; brushing with a stiff brush before the final coat of wax is dry will result in a more uniform colour. The possibilities are almost endless.

1 Mix only a very small quantity of yellow ochre artist's acrylic tube paint with white matt emulsion paint to achieve a soft, off-white colour. Scrub the wooden surface of the piece to be finished with a stiff wire brush to raise the grain. Sand away any furred or splintered wood with medium-grade glasspaper, then paint the wood with the off-white paint mixture.

2 Allow the paint to dry, then sand lightly to remove any rough surfaces and reveal areas of the underlying grain and saw marks. Apply a liberal quantity of light furniture wax and rub it well into the painted wood using a cotton rag.

3 When the wax is dry, sprinkle pinches of ash on to the timber. Dip the rag previously used for waxing into fresh wax and use it to work the ash into the surface of the wood. Experiment: the more ash you use, the darker the final finish. If it becomes too dark, add more wax and work the surface with your rag until the excess ash is removed. When you have a finish that satisfies you, leave the wax to dry.

4 When fully dry, polish the surface with a stiff brush and finish with a clean, dry cotton rag.

materials:

Rough-sawn or weathered softwood timber
Yellow ochre artist's acrylic tube paint
White matt emulsion paint
Light-coloured furniture wax
Fine wood or paper ash

equipment:

Heavy-duty wire brush
Medium-grade glasspaper
25mm (1in) paintbrush
Clean cotton rags
Stiff polishing brush

scumble glaze

Acrylic scumble glaze is a slow-drying transparent glaze that, when tinted with artist's acrylic tube paint and a little water, allows you to manipulate wet paint in various ways. (A more opaque glaze is achieved if mixed with white emulsion paint as well.) Specialist decorator's shops offer graining combs, textured rollers and brushes, such as stipplers, mottlers and floggers, but quite interesting results can be achieved using readily available household materials. Dragging the glaze with a dry brush gives a grained effect, while wiping with a dry rag produces a more irregular appearance. Experiment using a small natural sponge or a crumpled rag or plastic bag dipped in the glaze, applied in a sharp dabbing motion.

crackle glaze (craquelure)

This finish emulates the effects of old paint exposed to years of light and weather, in which a maze of cracks in the top coat of paint allows the underneath coat to show through. It is an ideal finish for contrasting colour paint finishes or where the cracks are to be emphasized with an ageing coloured wax or varnish.

The finish is achieved through the reaction of differing drying times of paints or varnishes. The simplest method is to apply a thin even coat of oil-based varnish over the item to be crackled; leave it to dry until only slightly tacky then brush over it a second coat of water-based varnish. Hair-like cracks will appear in the surface of the second coat as it dries. Experiment with drying times for different results – generally the dryer the first coat, the finer the resulting cracks. Proprietary water-based, spirit-based and varnish crackle glazes are available from hobby shops and specialist paint suppliers and are designed to work with finishes of the same base.

distressed paint finish

This popular finish is a useful and versatile technique for adding antiquity and character to wooden furniture and garden accessories, such as the Somerset trug (see page 28) and Farrier's box (see page 78).

Paint the item to be decorated in a single coat of matt emulsion paint. When the paint is dry, sand off sharp edges and all areas where naturally occurring wear would be evident, to reveal the underlying wood. Rub a good amount of furniture wax (light for light-coloured paint and antique brown for darker colours) into the painted surface with a cotton rag. Vigorous rubbing will dissolve the surface of the paint and areas of grain and solid colour will be created. To ensure a good finish always use sufficient wax on your rag to allow it to move easily over the paint. When the wax is dry, buff with a stiff brush and finish with a soft cotton cloth. This finish is not designed for permanent outdoor use. It will resist damp but distress-painted items should be brought indoors overnight and during wet conditions.

liming

Liming is most effective on hardwoods with a pronounced grain, such as oak or ash, and on softwoods that have been previously colour stained. Liming waxes are available from do-it-yourself stores and craft shops, but a very acceptable finish can be achieved on planed wood by simply painting with a diluted wash of white emulsion paint and wiping it off with a soft cloth while still wet so that the paint remains in the grain of the wood. When the paint is dry you can repeat the process for a lighter finish or sand it back with medium-grade wire wool to reveal more of the timber colour. Finish with light-coloured furniture wax or a matt or satin varnish.

timber

above *Creosote and white gloss paint have been used to preserve this enchanting old revolving summerhouse*

buying timber

Timber purchased from a timber merchant or do-it-yourself store may be sold as either "PAR" (planed all round) or rough sawn, sometimes called sawn or country cut. Rough-sawn timber can be bought untreated or already treated with preservative (tanalized). Rough-sawn timber is generally sold as true size but planed timber is often sold with measurements quoted before planing. Therefore timber planed from 75 x 25mm (3 x 1in) rough-sawn timber will be sold as "ex 75 x 25mm (3 x 1in) PAR". Its true planed size is more likely to be roughly 70 x 18mm (2¾ x ¾in).

Most commercially available softwood has been kiln dried to a moisture content of around 14 per cent but this moisture content will vary considerably according to the weather, ambient air moisture and the conditions in which the timber has been stored. Hardwoods generally have a closer grain structure and are more structurally stable, whereas softwoods are prone to bend, take up moisture easily and can expand and contract quite considerably dependent on their moisture content. Always select timber that has been properly stored, is relatively dry and shows no evidence of bowing across the grain (cupping) or splitting along the grain (shake).

Always store your timber flat and in the dry. Ideally, planks should be stacked on top of each other, separated from those above and below by strips of waste timber so as to allow free movement of air around the timber.

preserving timber

It is most important that timber used out of doors is properly protected against the depredations of weather and fungal wood rot. Softwoods are particularly susceptible to deterioration and special care must be taken to protect timber that is in permanent contact with soil or the ground. External wood protection has progressed from the traditional use of cattle urine, through lime and tar to the more recent preservatives such as creosote. One may only speculate as to which was the least pleasant to apply! Modern wood preservatives come in a wide range of formulations but are mostly sold as liquids, either ready to use or in concentrated form, generally to be diluted with water.

Many timber preservatives contain a stain or dye and are designed for either interior or outdoor use. It is essential that you select an outdoor formulated preservative for timber to be used outdoors, and always read and follow the manufacturer's instructions carefully. While most modern timber preservatives are safe to use, they can be dangerous to animals (and particularly fish). If you have ever spilled creosote on to bare skin you will know the importance of wearing gloves and the proper protective clothing.

You must always take care to ensure that the end grain of the timber is properly treated. If applying preservative by brush or spray, pay particular attention to saturate all sawn ends. It is advisable to dip the end grain of the timber in a container of preservative, leaving for sufficient time for the liquid to be absorbed into the wood.

Always use preservative on dry timber and, if working indoors, ensure that the work area is well ventilated. If working out of doors, screen the surrounding area and be careful not to spill preservative on grass or growing plants.

If you are constructing something for outdoor use, use already protected (tanalized) timber or treat it with preservative before assembly. Preservative applied after assembly may not penetrate all the joints and these will be vulnerable to subsequent rot. No preservative will protect timber for ever. To extend the life of wood used out of doors, it will be necessary to apply new preservative periodically. Teak and certain other hardwoods are used extensively for outdoor furniture; these should be treated periodically with teak oil or a similar oil to feed the wood and preserve its colour. Untreated hardwoods will fade in colour and are prone to splitting and cracking.

Oil-based gloss and satin (semi-gloss) paints provide effective protection for planed timber used out of doors, but do not be tempted to take any short cuts. To give complete protection use a recommended timber preservative followed by an oil-based wood primer, an oil-based undercoat and at least two coats of oil-based finishing coat.

There are two last important points. Firstly, timber in constant contact with soil or the ground remains damp and this will encourage rot. Raise any wooden planter or other timber construction off the ground with small stones or pieces of broken terracotta to allow air to circulate, and always line wooden containers with polythene or a similar material before filling with soil. Secondly, drilled holes, construction joints and nails and screws driven into timber all provide places that are susceptible to fungal attack. Pay particular attention to these areas when applying preservative.

left *A pond-side bench and table made from salvaged telephone poles and timber from a disused calf pen, and preserved with a coating of dark oak spirit-based preservative/wood stain*

ageing techniques

The colour and patina that ancient materials develop over time is quite lovely and the same look can be artificially recreated. Old painted wood that has been exposed to decades of wind, rain, light and air until the paint chips, cracks and wears and the exposed wood develops tone and texture bears little resemblance to its original state. Iron that has been painted and then rusts, is repainted and rusts again develops over time a rough and appealing appearance. Stone, tiles, clay bricks and terracotta pots attract moss and lichen and over time discolour with exposure to the elements.

We enjoy the beauty of "antique" doors and have assiduously collected many from old houses, farm sales and gardens over the years: some hundreds of years old, massively bound and studded in iron, others obviously the product of a craftsman's labour of love. We also have a store of old and weathered timber, rusted iron straps, hinges, door furniture and ancient terracotta, all of it salvaged over the years and kept in an outhouse, just waiting for an opportunity to be installed in some garden or interior scheme. A constant challenge is the need to blend the new with the old. Much of the charm of aged materials is that they have no solid or uniform colouring and we have experimented with a number of different techniques to give new materials the impression of age. Success comes only with experimentation but there are a few general tips that apply.

One of our particular successes is a wash that we use to colour and preserve new softwood timber for garden trellis and fencing in our garden. Commercially sold trellis is often finished in dark or harsh browns but we prefer an unobtrusive, soft colour that will blend into the natural stone of our house and not overawe the hues of the foliage around it. The wash is simple to make and we suggest you have handy plenty of rough-sawn timber scraps on which to test the colour. When dry, the wash will give a more solid colour than is apparent when first applied.

Half-fill a plastic bucket with water. Ideally, use a concentrated colourless wood preservative in the water, add a small quantity of white emulsion paint and mix thoroughly. Add a little black emulsion paint and a smaller quantity of blue. Mix again until the paint is completely dissolved. The wash should be a very watery grey colour and, when applied to bare wood, should not change its surface colour to any great extent. The effect of the wash when dry is to reduce the brashness of bare cut timber and to transform it to a soft grey weathered appearance, which will further mellow as the wood changes colour with time.

Old timber is seldom smooth so to emphasize the natural texture and grain of new wood, try charring the surface with a heat gun, or scouring along the wood with a heavy-duty wire brush to remove some of the soft grain and leave the harder grain proud. Use concentrated spirit-based wood stains applied liberally to parts of

above   *An arched timber door, leading to an early 19th-century walled garden, repaired over the years and showing little of its original colour*

above   *A 19th-century barred door, repaired with lattice trellis and with little of its original bright blue colour evident*

above   *A heavy ledge-and-brace softwood door in the brick wall of an Edwardian walled garden*

the surface to create areas of colour. Overlay different stains and washes and if one doesn't work cut it back with solvent or water. Always remember that wet washes, stains and paints dry to a different colour.

ageing metal

New metalwork is often sold galvanized or "japanned" (black painted). In order to remove these coatings and provide a softer matt finish that will oxidize over time or that can be painted, wrap the pieces to be aged in wire netting and place in a very hot fire. After ten minutes or so, remove the item from the fire with tongs and plunge into a tank of cold water or "quench" under a running tap.

Verdigris finish is another technique. There are specialist kits available for verdigris finishing but the technique is quite simple. Paint the item to be decorated in black matt emulsion paint (for an alternative finish try gold or bronze paint) and while it is drying make up a watery mixture of aqua coloured and white acrylic paint. When the base colour is dry, apply the watery aqua paint with a small natural sponge or a crumpled rag using a dabbing motion, or with a dry brush drawn across the metal surface. Your confidence in using this technique will increase with experience and allow you to create a finish that best suits the item being painted.

left *A finely made iron door latch on an old door rescued from a wrecker's yard, just waiting for reinstallation in a new site*

right *One of a pair of wrought-iron gates, made from decorative security grills, at one time installed inside the front door of a Welsh manor house*

far right *A verdigris finish on a modern wrought-iron garden bench*

ageing terracotta

The natural colour of today's machine-made terracotta is pleasing, if perhaps a little uniform and uninteresting. To accelerate the natural ageing process of the terracotta, you need to encourage natural moss and algae to start to work on what is often a very shiny surface and one on which these growths find it difficult to establish themselves. This ageing process works well and looks particularly good on pots with raised patterns.

materials
Terracotta pot
Natural yogurt
Liquid manure (optional)

equipment
50mm (2in) paintbrush
Spray mister

1 Paint the exterior and about 50mm (2in) down on the inside of your selected terracotta pot with natural yogurt or a mixture of yogurt and liquid manure. For country dwellers an extremely effective mixture can be made by mixing natural yogurt with the seepage from your compost bin or, if you keep horses, the manure heap! We have used organic yogurt in the belief that this will prove more attractive to naturally occurring mosses, algae and lichen, although there is no good reason why other yogurts cannot be used. However, fruit yogurts contain sugar which may attract unwanted wasps and flies.

2 Leave the pot in the open air for several weeks, preferably in a moist, warm environment, and dampen the surface of the pot periodically with water applied with a spray mister to encourage natural growths. Try not to touch the pot until the growth is established as this may wipe off the surface of the yogurt and result in a patchy appearance. The pot shown here has been exposed to the elements for just over four weeks.

useful addresses

specialist paint suppliers

Akzo Nobel Woodcare Ltd
Meadow Lane
St Ives
Cambridgeshire PE17 4UY

Tel: 01480 496868
Fax: 01480 496801

Sadolin and Sikkins range of specialist stains and paints

Dulux – ICI Paints
Dulux Advice Centre
Wexham Road
Slough
Berkshire SL2 5DS

Tel: 01753 550555
Fax: 01753 587218
website: www.dulux.com

Paints in thousands of colours including traditional period shades

Farrow and Ball Ltd
Uddens Trading Estate
Wimborne
Dorset BH21 7NL

Tel: 01202 876141
Fax: 01202 873793
email: farrow-ball@farrow-ball.co.uk
website: www.farrow-ball.com

National Trust range of paints

Hammerite Products Ltd
Prudhoe
Northumberland
NE42 6LP

Tel: 01661 830000
Fax: 01661 838100
email: info@hammerite.com
website: www.hammerite.com

Hammerite range of single-coat metal paints and anti-rust products

Paintworks
5 Elgin Crescent
London W11 2JA

Tel: 0171 792 8012
Fax: 0171 727 0207

Traditional paints, distempers, colour and limewashes. Specialist paint supplies and equipment

Potmolen Paint
27 Woodcock Industrial Estate
Warminster
Wiltshire BA12 9DX

Tel: 01985 213960

Suppliers of traditional and natural paints including distempers

timber and builder's suppliers

Jewson Ltd
Sutherland House
Matlock Road
Foleshill
Coventry CV1 4BL

Tel: 01203 669100
Fax: 01203 669188
email: marketing@jewson.co.uk
website: www.jewson.co.uk

Timber and building merchants, branches throughout the UK

wood protection products

Cuprinol Ltd
Addewell
Frome
Somerset BA11 1NL

Tel: 01373 465151
Fax: 01373 475010

Suppliers of timber protection and preservative products

Protek Products
Crowne Trading Estate
Charlton Road
Shepton Mallet
Somerset BA4 5QQ

Tel: 01749 344697
Fax: 01749 345572
email: protekproduct@compuserve.com
website:
       www.protektimbertreatments.co.uk

Fence paints and coloured preservative wood stains

Ronseal
Thorncliffe Park
Chapeltown
Sheffield S35 2YP

Tel: 0114 246 7171
Fax: 0114 245 5629

Wood protection products, stains and wood colours

stains, waxes and finishes

CW Wastnage Ltd
Burnham-on-Crouch
Essex CM0 8UA

Tel: 01621 785173
Fax: 01621 785393
email: wastnage@demon.co.uk

Waxes, teak oil, sealers and polishes

Hannants Traditional Waxes and Stains Ltd
248 Seabrook Road
Seabrook
Nr Folkestone
Kent CT21 5RQ

Tel: 01303 239932
Fax: 01303 230932
email: xlt32@pipex.co.uk

Waxes, stains and fillers

JW Bollom & Co Ltd
P O Box 78
Croydon Road
Beckenham
Kent BR3 4BL

Tel: 0181 658 2299
Fax: 0181 658 8672
email: Bollom.com.uk

Specialist waxes, stains, paints, varnishes and finishes, decorator's brushes and gilding supplies

Liberon Waxes Ltd
Mountfield Industrial Estate
New Romney
Kent TN28 8XU

Tel: 01797 367555
Fax: 01797 367575
email: liberon@demon.co.uk

Specialist waxes, stains, varnishes and finishes

information on wildlife

The British Trust for Ornithology
The Nunnery
Thetford
Norfolk IP24 2PU

Tel: 01842 750050
email: bto.staff@bto.org.uk

Information and publications on all aspects of ornithology. Nesting box plans, etc.

The Wildlife Trusts
The Green
Witham Park
Waterside South
Lincoln LN5 7JR

Tel: 01522 544400
Fax: 01522 511616
email: wildlifersnc@cix.compulink.co.uk
website: www.wildlifetrust.org.uk

Details of 46 local UK wildlife trusts

reclaimed materials

LASSCo Ltd
St Michael's
Mark Street
London EC2A 4ER

Tel: 0171 739 0448
Fax: 0171 729 6853
email: lassco@zetnet.co.uk
website: www.lassco.co.uk

Architectural antiques – garden ornaments, stonework, metalwork, lighting and fountains

Salvo
18 Ford Village
Berwick-upon-Tweed TD15 2QG

Tel: 01890 820333
Fax: 01890 820499
email: salvo@scotborders.co.uk
website: www.salvo.co.uk

Regional lists for the UK and mainland Europe of dealers in architectural antiques, antique garden ornaments and reclaimed materials

South West Reclamation
Gwilliams Yard
Edington
Nr Bridgwater
Somerset TA7 9JN

Tel: 01278 723173
Fax: 01278 722800

Walcot Reclamation
108 Walcot Street
Bath BA1 5BG

Tel: 01225 444404
Fax: 01225 448163

landscaping plants and shrubs

Ben Pike Garden Design
Round Trees
Smallway
Congresbury
North Somerset BS49 6AA

Tel: 01934 876355
Fax: 01934 835566

Garden and landscape design

Janet Walford
Upton Bridge Farm
Long Sutton
Langport
Somerset TA10 9NJ

Tel: 01458 241224
Fax: 01458 241186
email: walfor@globalnet.co.uk

Topiary in pots

Lands End Nurseries
Heath House
Wedmore
Somerset BS28 4UQ

Tel/Fax: 01934 713234

Wholesale nurseries

artists, potters and designers

Baytree Pottery
Baytree Cottage
71 Brent Street
Brent Knoll
Somerset TA9 4DX

Tel: 01278 760768

Hand-thrown terracotta pots and containers

Susie Gradwell
South View
Moorlynch
Nr Bridgwater
Somerset TA7 9BU

Tel: 01458 210018

Commissioned stencilling, mosaic and special paint effects

garden furniture and accessories

Drummonds of Bramley
The Kirkpatrick Building
25 London Road
Hindhead
Surrey GU26 6AB

Tel: 01428 609444
Fax: 01428 609445

Antique garden furniture, statuary, urns, etc.

Somerset Creative Products
Laurel Farm
Westham
Wedmore
Somerset BS28 4UZ

Tel: 01934 712416
Fax: 01934 712210
email: somprods@globalnet.co.uk

Somerset trugs, trays, chairs, benches, cupboards, tables, herb boxes, etc.

Sweerts de Landas
Antique Garden Ornaments
Dunsborough Park
Ripley
Woking
Surrey GU23 6AL

Tel: 01483 225366
Fax: 01483 224525
email: garden.ornaments@lineone.net.uk

Antique garden ornaments. Finials and figures in stone, lead, marble, cast iron and bronze

index

a

acetate, cutting stencils, 25
acrylic emulsion paints, 114
acrylic scumble glaze, 117
ageing techniques, 120–2
   crackle glaze (craquelure), 117
   distressed paint finish, 117
   metal, 121
   terracotta, 122
   timber 120–1
alabaster windows, 92
algae, ageing techniques, 122
aluminium furniture, 14
animals, 48, 51
antique gold pots, 86
arbours, 35
arches, 95
awning, 46–7

b

barrels, 67, 108
baskets, 14
bats, 48
   bat box, 56–7
benches, 13, 119
   cider bench, 20–1
birds, 48–51
   bird bath, 62–3
   bird tables, 50, 58–61
   evergreen topiary bird, 98–9
   nesting boxes, 52–3, 54–5
boxes:
   farrier's box, 78–9
   herb box, 79
   nesting boxes, 52–3, 54–5
butterflies, 51

c

cacti, 112
café chairs, 18–19
campaign chairs, 13
candles, 14, 113
   garden lights, 26–7
cane furniture, 14
canvas:
   hammock, 22–3
   staining, 115
cartridge paper, cutting stencils, 25
cast iron furniture, 14
chairs, 13
   colour, 113

decorated chairs, 18–19
cider bench, 20–1
clay pots, 66–9
   ageing techniques, 122
   antique gold pots, 86
   single-colour painted pots, 83
   terracotta wall planter, 70–1
   textured pots, 88–9
   white-washed pots, 87
climate change, 34
climbing plants, 92
   flowerpot topiary, 96–7
clock, window pane, 106–7
colour, 112–13
   ageing techniques, 120
   paints, 114
   stains, 115
concrete, fish box planter, 76–7
containers, 64–89
   colour, 113
   evergreen topiary bird, 98–9
   farrier's box, 78–9
   fish box planter, 76–7
   flowerpot topiary, 96–7
   flowerpots, 82–9
   herb box, 79
   orange box planter, 80–1
   patio planter, 72–3
   recycled wall planters, 102–3
   terracotta wall planter, 70–1
   window box/planter, 74–5
crackle glaze (craquelure), 117
creosote, 118
"crinkle crankle" walls, 34
cutting stencils, 25

d

deckchairs, 13
decorated chairs, 18–19
distressed paint finish, 117
dragging, scumble glaze, 117
dragonflies, 51

e

eating areas, 10–15
electricity:
   lighting, 14, 27
   water features, 108
emulsion paints, 114
   distressed paint finish, 117
evergreen topiary bird, 98–9

f

farrier's box, 78–9
fence stains, 115
fences, 35
finishes:
   crackle glaze (craquelure), 117
   distressed paint finish, 117
   liming, 117
   "ocean drift" finish, 116
   scumble glaze, 117
fish box planter, 76–7
flares, 27
flowerpots, 82–9
   antique gold pots, 86
   flowerpot topiary, 96–7
   single-colour painted pots, 83
   spatter finish plastic flowerpot, 84–5
   textured pots, 88–9
   white-washed pots, 87
flowers, wire heart, 100–1
focal areas, 66
fountains, 93
   slate fountain, 108–9
frogs, 51
fruit boxes, 80
furniture:
   cider bench, 20–1
   decorated chairs, 18–19
   eating areas, 13–14
   mosaic table top, 16–17

g

garden awning, 46–7
garden markers, 104–5
Garland, Eric, 35
glazes:
   crackle glaze (craquelure), 117
   scumble glaze, 117
global warming, 34
gloss paints, 119
gnomons, sundials, 44
gold pots, 86
Gradwell, Susie, 24
grasses, 112
gutter hoppers, 95

h

hammocks, 13, 22–3
hardwood:
   buying, 118
   café chairs, 18–19

preserving, 119
heart, wire, 100–1
hedgehogs, 48
hedges, 35
herb box, 79
herbicides, 51
hip tiles, recycled wall planters, 102–3
horizontal sundial, 42–5

i

insects, 48, 51, 52
iron:
   ageing, 120
   furniture, 14
ivy, flowerpot topiary, 96–7

l

lighting, 14
   garden lights, 26–7
liming, 117
linen, garden awning, 46–7
"Long Toms", 67, 82
Lonicera nitida, evergreen topiary bird, 98–9

m

markers, 104–5
marlin spikes, wind chime, 40, 41
Mathews, Ron, 76
metal:
   ageing techniques, 121
   café chairs, 18–19
micro-climates, 35
mirrors, 95
mock stone, fish box planter, 76–7
mosaic table top, 16–17

n

nesting boxes, 52–3, 54–5
   bird table, 58–61
newts, 51
night lights, 27
El Niño, 34

o

obelisks, 95
"ocean drift" finish, 116
   cider bench, 20–1
opaque stains, 115
orange boxes, 66
   orange box planter, 80–1

p

paints, 114
  ageing techniques, 120–1
  antique gold pots, 86
  crackle glaze (craquelure), 117
  distressed paint finish, 117
  liming, 117
  "ocean drift" finish, 116
  scumble glaze, 117
  single-colour painted pots, 83
  spatter finish plastic flowerpot, 84–5
parasols, 35
patio planter, 72–3
pergolas, 95
pesticides, 51
Pike, Ben, 108
pine furniture, 13
planters, 66
  fish box planter, 76–7
  orange box planter, 80–1
  patio planter, 72–3
  recycled wall planters, 102–3
  terracotta wall planter, 70–1
  window box/planter, 74–5
plants:
  evergreen topiary bird, 98–9
  flowerpot topiary, 96–7
  wire heart, 100–1
  see also containers
plastic furniture, 14
plastic pots:
  flowerpot topiary, 96–7
  spatter finish plastic flowerpot, 84–5
  textured pots, 88–9
polystyrene fish box planter, 76–7
ponds, 51, 108
pots:
  ageing techniques, 122
  antique gold pots, 86
  flowerpot topiary, 96–7
  recycled wall planters, 102–3
  single-colour painted pots, 83
  spatter finish plastic flowerpot, 84–5
  terracotta, 66–9, 82–3
  terracotta wall planter, 70–1
  textured pots, 88–9
  white-washed pots, 87
preserving timber, 118–19
primers, 114

r

rattan furniture, 14
recycled wall planters, 102–3
red oxide, 114
rope, textured pots, 88–9
rough-sawn timber, 118
rust-proofing paints, 19, 114

s

safari chairs, 13
safety, electricity, 108
screens, 35, 92
sculpture, 92, 93
scumble glaze, 117
seating, 10–15
  cider bench, 20–1
  decorated chairs, 18–19
shade, 35
sheds, colour, 113
shells, textured pots, 88–9
shrews, 51
single-colour painted pots, 83
slate:
  horizontal sundial, 42–5
  slate fountain, 108–9
softwood:
  buying, 118
  preserving, 118
Somerset trug, 28–31
spatter finish plastic flowerpot, 84–5
spirit-based stains, 115
stains, 115
  café chairs, 18–19
  wood preservatives, 118
steel:
  furniture, 14
  wind chimes, 40–1
stencilled garden tray, 24–5
stoneware urns, 66
sundials, 35
  horizontal sundial, 42–5
sunflower stencil, 24–5

t

table top, mosaic, 16–17
tanalized timber, 119
teak, 13, 119
terracotta, 66–9
  ageing techniques, 122

antique gold pots, 86
recycled wall planters, 102–3
single-colour painted pots, 83
terracotta wall planter, 70–1
textured pots, 88–9
white-washed pots, 87
textured pots, 88–9
tiles, 95
  border edgings, 95
  mosaic table top, 16–17
  recycled wall planters, 102–3
  terracotta wall planter, 70–1
timber, 110, 118–19
  ageing techniques, 120–1
  bat box, 56–7
  bird bath, 62–3
  bird nesting box, 54–5
  bird table, 58–61
  buying, 118
  café chairs, 18–19
  cider bench, 20–1
  containers, 66
  farrier's box, 78–9
  furniture, 13
  garden markers, 104–5
  herb box, 79
  liming, 117
  "ocean drift" finish, 116
  orange box planter, 80–1
  patio planter, 72–3
  preserving, 118–19
  Somerset trug, 28–31
  weather vane, 38–9
  window box/planter, 74–5
  window pane clock, 106–7
time:
  sundials, 42
  window pane clock, 106–7
tools, garden lights, 26–7
topiary, 113
  evergreen topiary bird, 98–9
  flowerpot topiary, 96–7
transparent stains, 115
trays, 14
  Somerset trug, 31
  stencilled garden tray, 24–5
trellis, 92, 120
trugs, 14
  Somerset trug, 28–31

antique gold pots, 86
recycled wall planters, 102–3
single-colour painted pots, 83
terracotta wall planter, 70–1
textured pots, 88–9
white-washed pots, 87

u

undercoat, 114

v

varnish, crackle glaze (craquelure), 117
verdigris finish, 121
voles, 51

w

wall planters:
  recycled, 102–3
  terracotta, 70–1
walls:
  shelter, 35
  trellis, 92
  wall decorations, 92
washes, ageing techniques, 120
water-based paints, 114
water-based stains, 115
water features, 51, 67
  slate fountain, 108–9
waterfalls, 108
waxes:
  distressed paint finish, 117
  liming, 117
weather, 32–7
weather vanes, 36–7, 38–9
white-washed pots, 87
wigwams, 95
"wild" gardens, 52
wildlife, 48–53
  bat box, 56–7
  bird nesting boxes, 52–3, 54–5
willow:
  screens, 14
  wigwams, 95
wind, 32, 35
wind chimes, 37, 40–1
window box/planter, 74–5
window pane clock, 106–7
wire heart, 100–1
wood see timber
wood stains, 115

y

yogurt, ageing techniques, 122

acknowledgements

Thank you to everyone at Octopus Publishing Group, especially Nina Sharman, Senior
Editor, who remained calm, and Geoff Borin, Executive Art Editor, for his imagination
and enthusiasm. Also Mel Yates, photographer, for his instinctive "eye".

Thank you also to: JW Bollom & Co Ltd for wax, liquid waxes and wood stains,
Dulux – ICI Paints for supply of paints and stains, Jewson Ltd for supply of timber,
hardware and builder's supplies, South West Reclamation for the loan of tiles,
slates and other items, Lands End Nurseries for the loan of plants for photography.

We are most grateful to those who assisted with projects, namely:
Susie Gradwell – stencil and mosaic work
Ron Mathews – fish box planter
Ben Pike – slate fountain
Janet Walford – topiary in pots

With thanks also to everyone for kindly lending their gardens for photography:
Susan Boss, Nicholas Brooking-Clark and Susie Gradwell, Andy and Claud Burn,
Mr and Mrs D Harris, Robert and Bridget McCrum, Ron and Judy Mathews, Derek and
Rosemary Menary, Peter and Rose Sanguinetti, Mr and Mrs D Tucker, Joe and Angela
Tucker, Janet Walford, Audrey Warner, Stuart and Ann Weichart.